Megan & Donny,

Happy cookm↑

Cheers

Beaver Creek '23

LOOI KIEN

RAPHAEL JOLY

SEBASTIEN COURR

SEBASTIAN JOLY AND STELLA

DANIEL JOLY

"SPECIAL THANKS TO MY LOVING WIFE, MY TWO SONS, MY STAFF AND ALL OF MY GUESTS WHO HAVE SUPPORTED ME THROUGHOUT THESE MANY YEARS."

Published by
Northstar Media Books

N★ NORTHSTAR MEDIA BOOKS

Text copyright © 2009 by
Daniel Joly

Food and Location photography
copyright © 2009 by
Charles Park

Library of Congress Catalog-in-
Publication Data available.

ISBN: 978-0-9819802-2-5

Manufactured in Singapore

10 9 8 7 6 5 4 3 2 1

Northstar Media, LLC
120 East Vermont Street
Indianapolis, IN 46204

www.northstarmediabooks.com

DANIEL JOLY
NOT JUST ANOTHER COOKBOOK

CONT

ENTS

MIRABELLE
DANIEL JOLY

If you know only one thing about me after putting down this book, I want it to be this: I am, first and foremost, a working chef. Some of those famous chefs you see on television never get dirty making food, and I suspect that a lot of them don't even work in a restaurant. I would never want to be a chef that people like to look at, but whose food nobody wants to eat. Working in the kitchen of Mirabelle, the restaurant I own in Beaver Creek, Colorado, and making food that delights my guests—that is what I enjoy most of all. Even after owning Mirabelle for more than a decade, my goal is still the same as it was on the first day I started: to please the customers who walk through the front door. And being in the kitchen allows me to make sure my customers get the quality I demand.

Don't get me wrong: The Food Network is fun to watch, and some of the chefs you see there are very good at what they do. I have been on television, too, and it is not all bad. When I was in my early 20s and still living in Belgium, the country where I was born, I worked in a two-star Michelin restaurant. Every year, an organization of Belgian master chefs (of which I am now a member) hosted a national competition to determine the country's best young chef, and in 1989 the owner of the restaurant where I worked needed one of his chefs to compete. I agreed to participate, not because I was seeking fame, but because I wanted an extra day off. As it turned out, I performed well, and later I found myself sitting in a big chair in front of a TV camera, doing a nationally televised interview on the evening news. The unexpected recognition paid well, because one of the judges of the competition, a chef at one of the best restaurants in Belgium, offered me a job, and those credentials would later help me secure a visa to work in the United States.

But celebrity can be a fragile thing. While it is nice to get recognition and the rewards it brings, I believe that, at the end of the day, it is more important for a chef to know how to run a kitchen than to know how to get attention. Being a celebrity chef and being a successful chef don't always go together. While being on television might sound cool, what really gives me pride is that during the 10-plus years since I took over Mirabelle, in 1999, our business has continually evolved while remaining very strong. That is what I consider to be a big accomplishment, especially since we are a mom-and-pop place that spends very little money on advertising. What makes us successful is people talking about us and telling their friends that they had a great meal at Mirabelle. And that comes from our constant focus on what we can do to improve. Simply put, Mirabelle is never going to be good enough for us. As a chef, I always strive to get better. That means never making food just to satisfy somebody

else. I make food that satisfies me, food that I think is good. Food is like fashion: It changes all the time, and staying current with dining trends is an important part of my routine. I respect the principle that the real value is in the flavor; if a technique doesn't enhance the flavor of a dish, I will not use it. Flavor should be the focal point, and that is a theme that runs through the food at Mirabelle and the recipes in this book.

That dedication to making food the right way is one of the main reasons why we can look back on 10-plus years of owning Mirabelle and say, "We're still here." But it is not the only reason. My wife Nathalie and I work hard and live humbly, and we raised our family in the apartment above the restaurant. Mirabelle isn't just our business; it is our home. Of course, owning a restaurant is the dream of many chefs. But it might be difficult for chefs born and raised in this country to understand what it means to a chef who has come from Belgium. In that country, probably 80 percent of the nice and well-established restaurants have been owned by the same families for three or four generations. For a young chef there to invest millions of dollars in opening a new restaurant, and have to compete with all those established restaurants, it is a big risk. As a young man starting my career there, it was very hard for me to see myself ever owning a place of my own. And if I had stayed in Belgium, I might never have.

In fact, my father was an architect, and he had mixed feelings about the idea of my being a chef in the first place. I told him I wanted to be a chef when I was a teenager, and his reply was, "No, no." When I persisted, he made me get a job in a fine restaurant. It was kind of a joke among him and his friends; they thought I would dislike the experience so much that it would discourage me. But it didn't work. I enrolled in a culinary apprenticeship program and started working in a restaurant where it was only me and two other

9

PICTURED (FROM TOP): JONATHAN FRECHLIN, MIRABELLE KITCHEN, PETER CASEY, DANIEL JOLY, MIRABELLE DINING ROOM

"I ALWAYS LIKED THE SETTING AND ATMOSPHERE HERE."

guys in the kitchen. I got a lot of hands-on experience with the chef, who took me on as a protégé. We had a bond, working together closely for two years, and my conviction to become a chef was as strong as ever.

By the time I finished school and had a few good experiences in Michelin-rated Belgian restaurants, my career path was, of course, decided. But Belgium is a small country (about the size of Maryland), and I wanted to try something different, explore someplace with more opportunities. At the time, my wife's parents owned a condo in Ft. Lauderdale, Florida, and we had visited a couple of times on vacation. I had always thought that people in the United States were very friendly—so nice that, in 1990, when I was 22 years old, we decided to come here to stay for a while. I found a job in an upscale restaurant in Charleston, South Carolina, but I only worked there for about a year before Hurricane Hugo shut the restaurant down for six months. Suddenly out of a job, I shopped around until, as luck would have it, I found another Belgian chef who worked here in the Vail Valley and helped me find the resort town of Beaver Creek. I was only in Colorado for about six months before I met Luc Meyer, a well-known local restaurateur who had opened the Left Bank, a classical French restaurant in Vail, and who, at the time, owned

Mirabelle. When I came to work at Mirabelle, in 1991, there was virtually no fine-dining competition in Beaver Creek. But as a result, Mirabelle really created the fine-dining scene here. There was just nobody else here at that time. If you were coming to this side of the valley, you were coming to Mirabelle at Beaver Creek .

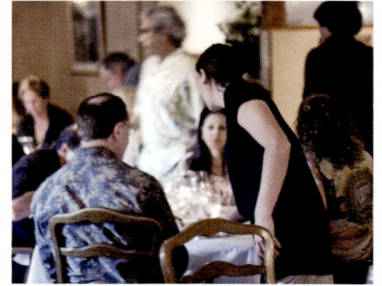

I always liked the setting and atmosphere here at Mirabelle. For one, the building is a historic landmark. Located on the site of the first homestead in the valley of Beaver Creak, it is a throwback to Old Colorado and the way people used to live before all the ski resorts came in. I just thought there was something very special about it. But it never once crossed my mind when I came to work here that I would end up owning it. As a matter of fact, not long after I started I was already thinking seriously about moving from the valley, and I had started to explore job opportunities in other states. But then my first son was born, and I realized that Beaver Creek would be a great place to settle down for a while and raise a family.

What appealed to me about working at Mirabelle was that the chef had a lot of control, and the kitchen showcased a very European style of cooking. Everything we served was nice and fresh, and each day we only prepped what we needed for that evening. I was seduced by that, because I had already worked at other places in this country where that wasn't the case. On the other hand, the style of cuisine at Mirabelle was quite a bit different in those days from what it is today. Shortly after I started working at Mirabelle, I changed the focus from classical French cuisine to food that better reflected my own background. I might be from Europe, but I have lived in America for a big part of my life. I have traditional French-style training, but I am still young enough to evolve with changing food trends. I can draw on things that I learned 20 years ago, while maintaining a willingness to learn new styles and techniques. Consequently, I wanted the cuisine at Mirabelle to be an open-minded fusion between different culinary styles and techniques. I describe it as contemporary, with a European flair.

"I RESPECT THE INGREDIENTS I USE TO PREPARE A DISH."

Fortunately, the changes we introduced at Mirabelle when I took over as chef were very well received—so much so, in fact, that one day a regular customer I had become friendly with, a very wealthy gentleman, took me aside and said, "Daniel, you're too talented to be working for somebody else," and he suggested that he might be able to help me get enough money together to buy the restaurant. I hadn't given much thought to owning Mirabelle before that, but suddenly it seemed like a real possibility. And it was exciting. So I went about figuring out what would be required to do it, and after discussing it with the owner, we agreed on a price. Of course I didn't have that kind of money in my wallet. So I went back to the wealthy customer and I went to the bank. And without delving into all the gritty details of how, I'll just say that two years later, in 1999, I had secured all the financing I needed. So I bought it. My main goal in those early days was just to stay in business, which was pretty stressful. It seemed like everything I owned, right down to my dirty underwear, was owed to the bank. I didn't even know if I could afford to buy a ticket back to Belgium if the restaurant failed. The fact that we celebrated our 10th year of owning the restaurant is truly a blessing.

The food at Mirabelle has evolved a great deal in the past decade, and it is still changing all the time. At present, we are very much influenced by the growing health consciousness of our diners. I think that historically, European people have longer understood that eating healthy means eating healthier portions. When you are eating, it takes your mind six minutes to realize that you're not actually hungry anymore; if you keep eating until your mind tells you that you're full, most of the time you're just stuffing yourself. More and more, people in the United States are motivated by eating healthy, too, and are not as insistent on getting big portions as they used to be. It is just not healthy to eat a 20-ounce piece of meat in one sitting. That is not the way I feed myself, it is not the way I feed my kids, and I don't want to feed my customers that way, either. When a guest has finished his meal, we want him to be able to go home and feel good about his dining experience, not have to loosen his belt and stretch out on the sofa because he is too full to move. That's not to say that I want people to leave the restaurant feeling hungry. If a big guy comes in and is still starving after he finishes his meal, we'll give him another plate. I don't have a problem with that. I would rather give him another plate and not charge him for it than feed everyone else too much and have them all feel overfull when they leave, or waste good food by throwing away what they can't eat.

For the most part, diners today seem to be looking for a higher grade of food and more balanced portions than they did when I started here. They want to have an experience with the food. It's about the pleasure of appreciating the flavor, not the pleasure of being full. As a result, I think the flavors at Mirabelle have become truer, more clean and more fresh. The reductions and sauces have a more contemporary flavor. It is my upbringing in the culinary tradition of Belgium that has, in large part,

THE VIEW FROM BELGIU[M]

helped me stay current with these new dining trends and influences. I have always said that the culinary tradition of a small country such as Belgium is similar to a large country such as the United States. Belgium is very much influenced by French food; Paris is only a two-hour car ride away. But if you drive for two hours in the other direction, you can be in Amsterdam. It is very easy for people in Belgium to travel to other countries. And because they travel so easily, they are influenced by the cuisines of many different countries. Of course, that is especially the case with chefs. With all those sister countries, you can pick up ideas from Germany, France, Holland and elsewhere, and bring them back and mix them up and call the food Belgian. That is why I compare Belgium to the United States. In a big country like this, where you have so many people coming in from everywhere else, all those influences create a unique national cuisine. In a country like France, which has such an established and serious culinary tradition, you run the risk of being made to burn your chef's coat if you prepare a classical dish differently. But I think chefs in both Belgium and the United States are more willing to experiment with food and the preparation of different dishes.

At the same time, though, I want to emphasize that while the food at Mirabelle is contemporary, I also want it to be authentic. I respect the ingredients I use to prepare a dish, and I want to preserve the true value of the food I'm using without doing anything too crazy to it. A rack of lamb should be a rack of lamb, not something you can't recognize. Of course, that means finding the best possible ingredients out there, and using produce when it is in season. I almost hesitate to mention that,

14

because it is just common sense. It seems like every time I open a cookbook these days, the chef is going on and on about how important it is to buy top-quality ingredients and in-season vegetables. And every time I read that, I think, "Well, of course. That's the only way you can make something nice." That's the way I was cooking when I was 20 years old and I still cook that way. I didn't have to come to America to learn that. Searching out the best ingredients is a challenge any chef should undertake. If you don't start with the right ingredients, how can you make anything good?

Using good ingredients is about being conscious of what you feed your customers. It's about an honest way of doing business. But using the best ingredients doesn't necessarily mean using those that are expensive or precious. It doesn't mean you have to have caviar or truffles in every dish. It's easy to present yourself as a big-time chef when you use ingredients such as truffles, because nobody can afford the food. Everybody can be a great chef using caviar and truffles. That's not where I get my kicks. It is more rewarding for me to make something delicious with modest ingredients such as, say, artichokes, or oft-forgotten root vegetables such as red beets and salsify. They may be humble, but when you can bring them to a level where they are sexy to eat because of the presentation and application—that is exciting. Have you ever discovered a great wine, and it seemed to taste that much better because you bought it at a good price? In the same way, using modest ingredients is one way we keep the restaurant approachable and make sure that a meal here is a great value. Everyone, regardless of age or class, should be able to have a nice meal once in awhile, without having to spend a thousand dollars. And that is what we try to offer.

That is the same approach I wanted to take with this book: I wanted it to be accessible. We have probably done thousands of different recipes at Mirabelle over the years, and I like to think of the ones in this book as the ones that stand out, an inventory of particularly good dishes. Some originated in Europe, and some are from the United States. Some are rustic, and some are seasonal. But what I hope they all share is that if a home chef looks at any one of them, he can say, "I might try that." I am not interested in using these recipes to demonstrate what a skilled chef I am, if it means no one else will attempt to make the recipes. I don't want to recommend ingredients so complicated that nobody can find them. If you can't take the book into the kitchen and use it, then what is the point? That would be like having a nice car you can never drive. I want to encourage people to try new things in the kitchen by sharing the dishes that I think people will find accessible. Cooking is like riding a bicycle. The more you cook, the more comfortable you will get. After a while, your mind might even start to mix flavors automatically, and you won't even need to use the recipes as often. That's okay. I encourage you to experiment. But if there's one thing I have learned, it is not to compromise on the quality. We never have at Mirabelle, and we have more than 10 good years to show for it.

"CHEFS IN BELGIUM AND THE U.S. ARE WILLING TO EXPERIMENT."

COOKII

WITH BE

Mioelle
Dan Joly

bell

You will probably notice that a good number of the recipes in this book include beer. Ten years ago, you never would have seen a dish flavored with beer on the menu at Mirabelle, because it didn't fit with what we were doing. But a few years ago, I started introducing a handful of beer-related recipes in cooking classes and demonstrations, and people reacted really well. So I thought, "Why don't I incorporate that into the food at my restaurant from time to time?" I've become a lot more willing to play with beer in some of the dishes at Mirabelle than I was before.

I suspect that a lot of people in America might, at first, be intimidated by the thought of cooking with beer. Most home chefs would have no problem reducing wine to cook with, but they usually just keep the beer in the cooler without ever thinking about cooking with it. It is a relatively unknown practice in this country, with the exception, maybe, of boiling bratwurst in it or using it in waffle dough.

What you have to understand, though, is that in Belgium cooking with beer is recognized as much as cooking with wine is in France. It is nothing new at all. In fact, we have been cooking with beer in Belgium for 400 years now. My parents cooked with beer. It is just something we have in our roots. And it is my belief that cooking with beer can be even more sophisticated than cooking with wine. Wine, of course, starts with the grape, which is sweet. And when you reduce a wine, it gets even

17

sweeter. Cabernet and pinot noir, for example, are distinctive wine-grape varieties. But if you reduce both of them, and then put a finger in each one to taste it, you have to be a world champion connoisseur to distinguish the difference because all of the complexity has been cooked away. Beer, on the other hand, does not lend itself to reduction due to its inherent bitterness. If you reduce a beer, all of the flavors get condensed, and you end up with an almost aggressive flavor. Then there is virtually no amount of sugar you can add to make it sweet again. Beer is just a much different article than wine, and you have to be a little more ingenious in the way you use it.

If you think of beer as another flavor to use in your recipes, then it can be a very interesting ingredient to cook with. It is important to consider the flavor of the beer you're using—and beer, because it comes in nearly endless varieties, has countless flavors—and then ask yourself how best to impart that flavor on the dish. That is why cooking with beer is, to me, almost more intriguing than cooking with wine, because wine has limits to what you can do with it. But the possibilities of cooking with beer can be endless because you're using its flavor, almost as though it is a spice or seasoning, like paprika. Take the Belgian beer Hoegaarden: In that beer alone you've got a complex array of ginger, orange and other citrus flavors. Using a beer like that gives you a whole new set of tools in the kitchen.

As far as how to approach using beer in food, I am fortunate to have been born in a country where it is a common practice, so I think my mind might work a little faster than that of someone who is not as familiar with beer as an ingredient. There are some things I just don't try (reducing beer, for example) because I know they won't come out right; I know what works and I know what to stay away from. Because of my background, I have an inclination for what to cook beer with—such as cherries with beer, which I already know is magic. Having that knowledge makes it a little easier for me when I want to create a dish such as, say, elk with cherries and beer.

In general, when I am trying to create a dish using beer, I start by remembering that it is, essentially, 80 percent water and 20 percent spice. So how can I use that water and spice? I like to use beer in ways that I consider to be more contemporary, even avant-garde. For example, steaming fish with beer gets the flavor of the beer inside of the fish. Beer has the quality of being a nice, refreshing liquid when you're thirsty, and that is what I try to emphasize: the refreshing aspect of beer, while trying to stay away from the bitter taste. I might make a sauce, reducing it with, say, shallots and ginger, until it is just a little too thick; then I will add beer to that, which adds the flavor of fresh beer.

Ultimately, I think it is my job as a chef to look at the whole of the preparation and add a twist in a way that makes the dish modern and keeps it consistent with the style of cuisine we feature at Mirabelle. It would be quite possible, in fact, to write an entire book about cooking with beer, which is not my intent. But I hope the recipes I have included in this book offer a nice sampling.

THE VIEW FROM BELGIUM

An appetizer should be something that gets you in the mood for eating. For that reason, at Mirabelle we like to keep the flavors clean so that you will want to eat more after you have finished the appetizer. The dish shouldn't be overpowering because something else is coming after it. We also like to highlight dishes with unique applications among the appetizers, things that might not be pleasant if you ate too much of them, but that, in the right portions, are very nice. Examples are foods that are marinated instead of cooked, such as the Buffalo Tartare (recipe, page 22); it has a very refreshing flavor but probably wouldn't be appropriate for a larger-sized main course (eating 8 ounces of raw meat just wouldn't be right). Foie gras, as in the Hot Foie Gras with Blueberries and Blood Orange Reduction (recipe, page 24), is another good example. While it is delicious, it is rich and dense enough that eating too much of it in one sitting might throw off the balance of the meal. I generally approach appetizers as reduced portions of main courses, and it's not unusual for guests at Mirabelle to order a couple of appetizers and eat them as a main course because they like the idea of not having all the starches or vegetables that they might get with the standard main-course dishes.

BUFFALO TARTARE

MAYONNAISE

2 egg yolks

1 teaspoon Dijon mustard

1 tablespoon plus 1 teaspoon salt

1 cup vegetable oil

1 teaspoon cayenne pepper

1 tablespoon ketchup

1 tablespoon Worcestershire sauce

1 tablespoon lemon juice

1 tablespoon horseradish

TARTARE

5 ounces ground buffalo meat

Mayonnaise (recipe above)

Salt and pepper, to taste

1 wonton wrapper

Microgreens, to garnish*

Serves 4

Microgreens are tangy and tender lettuce and mustard greens that are chopped off young, usually when they are only an inch or so high and a few weeks old. Most grocers do not carry microgreens. You can substitute another more readily available variety of greens or, better yet, order microgreens online from various providers including www.sungrownorganics.com.

Most French chefs will tell you that "real" tartare is cut by hand, but I prefer a coarse-ground meat, just as my mother used to prepare it. I like to use buffalo rather than beef because it is much leaner and lower in cholesterol. Many grocery chains now carry buffalo, but if you can't find it there, your specialty meat market should have plenty on hand. If you simply can't find it, this recipe works just as well with high-quality lean beef.

1. In the bowl of a stand mixer, use the whisk attachment to mix the egg yolks with the Dijon mustard and salt. Mix together well until all the ingredients are completely incorporated. While continuing to mix, slowly drizzle in the oil until you have a mayonnaise-like consistency (thick, rich and opaque in appearance). Use more oil if needed to achieve the correct consistency. If you do not have a stand mixer, a household blender will work as well.

2. Stir in the remaining ingredients to combine well. Refrigerate the mayonnaise until time to use.

3. Preheat oven to 350 degrees.

4. In a mixing bowl, combine the ground buffalo and the mayonnaise. (You likely won't need to add all of the mayonnaise; rather, use just enough to bind the meat and create a smooth texture.) Season to taste with salt and pepper.

5. Mold the wonton wrapper (I like to use the store-bought variety) into a cup shape and bake it in the 350-degree oven for 4-5 minutes (or until it is golden in color and holding its cup shape). Let the wonton cool before you add a portion of the tatare (so as not to cook the tartare inadvertently).

6. Place the tartare-filled wonton on a plate with some additional tartare and fresh microgreens.

HOT FOIE GRAS WITH BLUEBERRIES AND BLOOD ORANGE REDUCTION

CHAMPAGNE VINAIGRETTE

1 shallot, finely chopped

¼ cup champagne vinegar

½ cup grapeseed oil

¼ cup avocado oil

Salt and pepper, to taste

HOT FOIE GRAS WITH BLUEBERRIES AND BLOOD ORANGE REDUCTION

8 ounces (about 2 cups) blueberries

½ cup sugar

1 tablespoon butter

4 gelatin sheets

16-18 ounces fresh Grade-A foie gras

1 cup blood orange juice

1 vanilla bean

ASSEMBLY

2 ounces mixed baby greens (about ½ cup, lightly packed)

2 tablespoons champagne vinaigrette (recipe above)

Serves 4-6

1. Add all of the vinaigrette ingredients to a mixing bowl and whisk until they are thoroughly incorporated. Reserve. (This recipe will yield far more vinaigrette than you'll need for this dish; unused dressing will keep in the refrigerator for 10 days or so.)

2. In a small saucepan, mix the blueberries with 2 teaspoons of the sugar and all of the butter. Cook over medium heat until the sugar is melted (about 2 minutes).

3. Place the gelatin sheets in a bowl of cold water long enough to soften them. Remove them from the water and pat them dry with a lint-free towel. Add the sheets to the blueberry mixture and stir until the gelatin is completely dissolved.

4. Divide the blueberry gelatin mixture among 4-6 small cups in a silicone mold or muffin pan. Chill in a refrigerator for 1 hour.

5. While the blueberry gelatin mixture is cooling, slice the foie gras into 4-6 slices about ¼-inch thick (about 3-4 ounces per serving). Refrigerate them until just before searing.

6. In a small saucepan over medium-high heat, heat the blood orange juice along with the remaining sugar. Split the vanilla bean lengthwise and scrape the pulp into the saucepan. Reduce this mixture by half.

7. Preheat a medium-size sauté pan over high heat.

8. While the sauté pan is preheating, dress the mixed baby greens with the champagne vinaigrette, tossing them until they are lightly coated. Reserve.

9. Add the foie gras to the hot sauté pan and sear each slice on both sides (about 2-3 minutes per side, depending on the thickness).

10. To assemble the dish, place a small circle of the blueberry gelatin on the center of a serving plate; place a slice of the foie gras on top of the gelatin. Pour some of the blood orange reduction over the foie gras, then place a small portion of the dressed greens on top of the foie gras. Serve immediately.

VEAL CARPACCIO WITH CILANTRO HERB SALAD

½ teaspoon coriander seeds

4 tablespoons hazelnut oil

2 tablespoons grapeseed oil

1 bunch fresh chervil

3 small sprigs tarragon

3 basil leaves

16 micro cilantro leaves*

4-6 ounces top round veal, trimmed

Salt and pepper, to taste

¼ cup freshly shaved Parmesan

Toast Dentelle, to garnish**

Serves 4

*Microgreens (including micro cilantro) are tangy and tender lettuce and mustard greens that are chopped off young, usually when they are only an inch or so high and a few weeks old. Most grocers do not carry microgreens. You can substitute another more readily available variety of greens or, better yet, order microgreens online from various providers including www.sungrownorganics.com.

**Toast Dentelle is simply sliced, lightly toasted baguette or bread.

1. Using a peppermill, grind the coriander seeds into a small bowl.

2. Add the hazelnut oil and grapeseed oil to the coriander and set aside to marinate for 2 hours.

3. After 2 hours, strain the coriander mixture through a fine-mesh strainer, reserving the oil. Discard the coriander.

4. Chop the chervil, tarragon, basil and cilantro and then place them in a separate bowl.

5. Slice the veal very thinly with a sharp knife and arrange the slices on a chilled plate. (Putting the veal in the freezer for 20 minutes beforehand makes it easier to slice.) Drizzle the coriander oil over the veal and season it to taste with salt and freshly ground pepper. Sprinkle the chopped herbs and shaved Parmesan over the veal and serve chilled. Garnish with the warm toast Dentelle.

RED BEET GNOCCHI WITH COLORADO GOAT CHEESE CREAM AND FRIED BABY ARUGULA

GNOCCHI

2 Yukon gold potatoes

2 red beets

Sea salt (or kosher salt), to taste

3 egg yolks

1 cup all-purpose flour

Salt and pepper, to taste

Grated nutmeg, to taste

Extra-virgin olive oil, as needed

Butter, as needed

GOAT CHEESE

1 cup soft goat cheese

1 cup heavy cream

Juice of 1 lemon

½ cup freshly chopped chives

Salt and pepper, to taste

FRIED ARUGULA

Vegetable oil, for deep-frying

1 lightly packed cup baby arugula

PARSLEY OIL

½ bunch parsley

½ cup vegetable oil

Serves 6

Most people find that making gnocchi can be a bit tricky. It is important that the consistency of the dough is just right, particularly with this recipe, since potatoes and beets each have a different water content. The recipe calls for 1 cup of flour, which is a good estimate. The dough is the correct consistency when it holds a ball shape and does not stick to your hands, so add the flour in increments until you achieve this result.

1. Preheat oven to 350 degrees.

2. Season the potatoes and red beets to taste with sea salt and then wrap them in aluminum foil. Roast in the 350-degree oven until they are tender (30-40 minutes; check tenderness using the tip of a knife). When they are tender, remove the potatoes and beets from the oven and unwrap them. When they are cool enough to handle, skin the potatoes and beets and pass them through a food mill or ricer. (If you do not have a food mill or ricer, you can use a fork or handheld masher.)

3. Place the milled potatoes and beets in a mixing bowl and add the egg yolks and flour. Mix them together well and then season the gnocchi dough to taste with salt, pepper and ground nutmeg.*

4. On a lightly floured work surface, roll the dough into a long cylindrical shape with your hands and then cut it, at a slight angle, into ½-inch-long cylinders. Use a fork to impress nice lines into the individual gnocchi pieces. Dust a sheet pan with flour (to prevent sticking) and lay the portioned gnocchi on the pan.

5. Grease a second sheet pan with olive oil.

6. Prepare a pot of boiling water with a pinch of salt. Cook the gnocchi in the boiling water for only a couple of minutes. When the gnocchi rise to the surface, remove them and set them in a cold-water bath to stop the cooking process. Transfer the cooled gnocchi from the bath to the oiled sheet pan and then place them in the refrigerator while you prepare the goat cheese and arugula.

7. Mix the goat cheese with the heavy cream and lemon juice until you achieve a creamy, rich consistency. (It is best to add the cream a few tablespoons at a time to insure that the mixture does not become too thin.) Add the chopped chives, season to taste with salt and pepper, and then stir the mixture well to incorporate the ingredients. Reserve.

8. Pour the vegetable oil into a deep-fryer and heat it to 250 degrees. Deep-fry the arugula in the hot oil until the leaves are transparent and crunchy. This process takes just a few minutes. (If a deep-fryer is not available, use a deep-sided sauté pan with about an inch of vegetable oil. Make sure the oil is very hot and then place the arugula in the oil until it curls and becomes firm.) Remove the arugula with a spider or slotted spoon and place it on a paper towel-lined plate to drain.

9. While the arugula is draining, blend the parsley with the vegetable oil. Strain the oil and discard the parsley solids. Reserve.

10. Sauté the gnocchi in butter in a warm pan over medium heat, just long enough to heat the gnocchi through and give them a crisp outer layer.

11. To assemble the dish, place the goat cheese cream in the center of a bowl and then put some of the sautéed gnocchi on top of it. Garnish with the deep-fried arugula and drizzle parsley oil around the plate.

TOMATO TART

CRUST (FOR ONE TART)

1 cup flour

1 egg

⅔ cup butter

2½ tablespoons sugar

1½ teaspoons salt

SALAD

2 large, ripe heirloom tomatoes, quartered

½ red onion, thinly sliced

½ cup fresh, pitted kalamata olives, sliced

12 fresh basil leaves

¼ cup red wine vinegar

½ cup extra-virgin olive oil

¼ cup avocado oil*

Salt and pepper, to taste

TART FILLING (FOR TWO TARTS)

1 onion, sliced

Extra-virgin olive oil, as needed

2 carrots, peeled and sliced

3 stalks celery, sliced

1 red bell pepper, sliced

1 leek, sliced

3 cups V8 juice

4¼ cups tomato puree

Salt and pepper, to taste

Sugar, to taste

4 egg yolks

Serves 10

Avocado oil is known to be one of the healthiest oils due to its high levels of monounsaturated fats and vitamin E. Although it is not heated in this recipe, avocado oil has an unusually high smoke point of 491 degrees Fahrenheit (255-degrees Celsius).

**To blind bake, line the tart shell with parchment paper and then place dried beans or pie weights on the paper before placing it in the oven. Remove the paper and beans or pie weights after taking the tart shell out of the oven.*

I like to use Colorado tomatoes in peak season or organic heirloom tomatoes. Since tomatoes provide the primary flavor in this recipe, using a great-tasting variety will produce the best result. The recipe for the tart filling will yield enough for two tarts, so you'll need to make two crusts (the recipe below is for a single crust).

1. Preheat oven to 350 degrees.

2. Put all of the crust ingredients in the bowl of a stand mixer with the dough-hook attachment and mix until the dough is smooth (about 3-4 minutes).

3. On a floured surface, roll out the dough to 12 inches in diameter and about ⅛-inch thickness. Carefully transfer it to a 9-inch tart pan and blind bake the shell in the 350-degree oven until it is golden brown (about 10 minutes). Reserve.**

4. For the salad, combine the tomatoes, onion, olives and basil in a large mixing bowl.

5. In a separate bowl, vigorously whisk together the vinegar and oils. Pour over the salad to coat it lightly and then season it to taste with salt and pepper. Reserve.

6. Preheat oven to 375 degrees.

7. In a wide sauté pan over medium heat, sauté the onion in extra-virgin olive oil until it is soft and translucent.

8. Add the carrots, celery, red bell pepper and leek to the pan and continue to sauté until the vegetables are very soft (about 2 minutes).

9. Place all of the cooked vegetables into a blender (working in batches if necessary) and add the V8 juice and tomato puree. Season to taste with salt, pepper and sugar. Blend everything together and transfer to a mixing bowl. Measure out 4 cups of the filling for each tart. After the mixture has cooled, add 2 egg yolks to each 4-cup portion and mix well.

10. Pour the filling into the tart shells and bake in the 375-degree oven until cooked through (15-20 minutes).

11. Garnish the tarts with the tomato salad. You may serve the tarts at room temperature or cold.

LES PETITES MOULES AUX LEGUMES ET HOEGAARDEN BIÈRE

LES PETITES MOULES AUX LEGUMES ET HOEGAARDEN BIÈRE

½ cup butter

2 shallots, small dice

1 stalk celery, small dice

1 carrot, small dice

1 leek, small dice

2 cups Hoegaarden beer

4½ pounds fresh "PEI" mussels, cleaned*

1 laurel (bay leaf)

1 bouquet lemon thyme

Salt and pepper, to taste

FRENCH FRIES

Potatoes (as many as you like)

Vegetable oil, for deep-frying

Salt, to taste

Serves 4

Prince Edward Island mussels, or "PEI" mussels, are known for their quality. If they are not available, use another variety of fresh, high-quality mussels.

1. In a large pan with 2 tablespoons of the butter, cook the shallots, celery, carrot and leek until they are tender (about 6 minutes).

2. Add the beer, mussels, laurel and lemon thyme to the pan and cover, cooking them until all of the mussels have opened. (Discard any mussels that do not open.) Transfer the mussels and vegetables to a bowl and strain the cooking broth back into the pan. Bring the liquid to a boil and stir in 2 tablespoons of the butter to obtain a smooth sauce. Season to taste with salt and pepper.

3. Pour the sauce over the mussels. Serve with french fries (recipe follows) or rice.

4. To make french fries, peel the potatoes and then cut them into sticks ½ inch wide by 2½ inches long. Rinse them in water and dry them on a clean cloth.

5. Precook the french fries in a deep-fryer in 300-degree oil for 5 minutes. Remove them from the fryer.

6. Raise the temperature of the oil to 390 degrees. Recook the fries until they are golden in color (about 4 minutes). Remove them from the oil and spread them out on a paper towel-lined tray to drain. Season them to taste with salt and serve immediately.

CRAB CAKES WITH COLORADO CORN

MAYONNAISE

2 egg yolks

1 tablespoon Dijon mustard

1 tablespoon salt

1 cup vegetable oil

SPICY AVOCADO EMULSION

1 ripe avocado, halved, pitted and meat
  scooped out

½ cup sour cream

Juice of ½ lemon

1 pinch cayenne pepper

1 pinch salt

CRAB CAKES

1 pound lump crabmeat

½ cup seasoned bread crumbs

2 eggs

⅔ cup chopped corn

3 tablespoons clarified butter

Vegetable oil, for frying

Salt and pepper, to taste

SALAD

⅓ cup red wine vinegar

1 cup avocado oil*

4 cups mixed baby greens

Serves 4

**Avocado oil is known to be one of the healthiest
oils due to its high levels of monounsaturated fats
and vitamin E.*

1. In the bowl of a stand mixer, use the whisk attachment to mix the egg yolks with the Dijon mustard and salt. Mix together well until all of the ingredients are completely incorporated. While continuing to mix, slowly drizzle in the oil until you have a mayonnaise-like consistency (thick, rich and opaque in appearance). Use more oil if needed to achieve the correct consistency. If you do not have a stand mixer, your household blender will work as well. Refrigerate the mayonnaise until you are ready to use it.

2. To make the spicy avocado emulsion, combine all of the emulsion ingredients and mix until smooth using a food processor or stand mixer. Reserve.

3. Remove any shell or cartilage from the crabmeat. Using a fork, combine the crabmeat, bread crumbs and eggs in a large mixing bowl. Refrigerate for at least 1 hour for easier handling and then mold into 4 patties. Cover just one side of each crab cake with the chopped corn, applying it like a crust (be sure to do this on only one side of each cake).

4. Add a thin layer of clarified butter to the bottom of a large skillet over medium heat. Place the cakes (corn side up) in the butter, cover the pan and cook the crab cakes on one side until golden brown.

5. While the crab cakes are cooking, make the salad. Pour the red wine vinegar and the avocado oil into a mixing bowl and whisk until they are well combined. Toss the salad leaves in the dressing. Reserve.

6. Remove the crab cakes from the pan and drain them on a paper towel.

7. To assemble the dish, pour a little of the spicy avocado emulsion onto each plate, set the crab cake on top of it and then arrange some of the salad on top of that. Serve immediately with the fresh mayonnaise.

SOUP+SAL

PIZZA+PAS

I like to think that the selection of recipes in this chapter offers a perfect example of how the menu at Mirabelle combines classical dishes from the Old World with dishes that are influenced by today's more contemporary way of eating. In addition to traditional recipes for Lobster Bisque (recipe, page 38) and Duck Confit Salad with Poached Egg (recipe, page 52), for example, you will find recipes for more inventive dishes such as the Chilled Melon Soup with Diced Prosciutto Ham (recipe, page 44) and the Thai Papaya Salad with Sautéed California Prawns (recipe, page 48). It is also important to note that while all of these recipes might fall into the second chapter of the book, I certainly do not mean to imply that they are only appropriate as the second course of a meal. Because many of them call for modest portions, they would work well as first courses, especially the soups and salads. And I can just as easily imagine readers of this book using some of these dishes as main courses—for example, by increasing the portion size of the Chanterelle Ragout with Acorn Squash Ravioli (recipe, page 65). How you approach serving many of these dishes might depend largely on the time of year. In the summertime, I could see myself eating just the Artichoke Salad (recipe, page 56) as a main course, and maybe starting with the Cold Gazpacho Soup (recipe, page 42). It's not necessary to set rules on how you use these dishes. The important thing is that you enjoy eating them.

LOBSTER BISQUE

2 lobsters

3 tablespoons olive oil

1 carrot, chopped

½ onion, chopped

1 small stalk celery, chopped

1 clove garlic, chopped

½ bulb fennel, chopped (just the bulb)

1 tomato, chopped

Star anise, 3 stars or to taste

Thyme, 4 sprigs or to taste

Basil, 4 leaves or to taste

Salt and pepper, to taste

2 tablespoons cognac

½ cup white wine

1 cup fish stock

1 cup water, plus more as needed

2 quarts heavy cream, or as needed

Arrowroot or cornstarch, as needed, to
    thicken the soup

Whipped cream, to garnish

Chopped parsley, to garnish

Serves 4

*If you don't have a steamer, boil the live lobsters in
lightly salted water, 3 minutes per pound.*

1. Preheat oven to 450 degrees.

2. Remove the head from each lobster and crush it using a meat mallet to maximize the amount of flavor extracted when making the stock. (Set the rest of the lobster aside.) Place the crushed heads in a baking dish or on a sheet pan and bake them in the 450-degree oven for 20 minutes. Remove them from the oven and reserve.

3. Steam the rest of the lobsters by bringing just over 1 inch of water to a boil in the bottom of a steamer pot. Add the lobsters to a steamer basket and place them in the pot to steam for 15 minutes (or until the meat is firm). Remove them from the pot, allow them to cool and then remove the meat from the tail and claws and set aside.*

4. In a saucepan over medium heat, add the olive oil and then sauté the carrot, onion, celery, garlic, fennel and tomato until the vegetables become soft and their colors develop (about 4-6 minutes).

5. Season the vegetables to taste with the star anise, thyme, basil, and salt and pepper; cook them for another 2 minutes.

6. Add the cognac, white wine, fish stock, 1 cup water and the crushed lobster head to the pan and cook at a low simmer for 45 minutes.

7. Remove the pan from the heat and strain the mixture, keeping the broth and discarding the solids. Add an equal amount of cream to the broth (for 1 cup of broth add 1 cup of cream). Cook the soup again for 15 minutes to reduce slightly.

8. Thicken the bisque with equal parts water and arrowroot or cornstarch as needed (dissolving the arrowroot or cornstarch in the water to create a slurry before adding it to the soup). Season to taste with salt and pepper, if necessary.

9. Pour the soup into 4 shallow bowls and garnish each bowl with a spoonful of whipped cream, a spoonful of chopped parsley and a small piece of the cooked lobster.

CORN CHOWDER

1 tablespoon butter

1 pound potatoes, peeled and diced

8 ounces onion (about 2 onions),
   thinly sliced

1½ teaspoons chili powder

2½ cups vegetable stock

2½ cups milk

Salt and pepper, to taste

8 ounces fresh haddock filet, skinned and
   broken into bite-sized pieces

8 ears fresh corn, cut from the cob

4 ounces prawns, cooked and peeled

½ cup chopped parsley, to garnish

½ cup chopped red bell pepper, to garnish

Serves 4-6

For me, this soup is always better when you serve it the next day. Let the ingredients marinate together overnight for a more full-bodied flavor.

1. Heat the butter in a large saucepan over medium heat. Add the potatoes, onion and chili powder to the pan and sauté just until the vegetables are softened (2-3 minutes).

2. Pour the stock and milk into the pan and lightly season to taste with salt and pepper. Bring the liquid to a boil, raising the heat as necessary, and then cover and steam for 10 minutes.

3. Add the haddock and corn kernels to the pan. Return the liquid to a boil and then cover and simmer until the potatoes are tender and the fish begins to flake apart. (Skim the surface as necessary to remove any foam.)

4. Stir in the prawns, parsley and the red bell pepper and then adjust the seasoning to taste with salt and pepper.

COLD GAZPACHO SOUP

3 ripe tomatoes (Colorado summer
   tomatoes, if available), peeled
   and chopped

2 cucumbers, peeled, seeded and chopped

1 red onion, chopped

3 cloves garlic, chopped

¼ jalapeño, chopped, membrane and
   seeds removed

Salt and pepper, to taste

1 avocado, diced, to garnish

2 basil leaves, chiffonade, to garnish

Serves 4

When possible, I like to source these ingredients from local Colorado farms. If you like your gazpacho on the coarse side, use a meat grinder instead of a blender.

1. Combine the tomatoes, cucumbers, onion, garlic and jalapeño in a large bowl and then cover with a plastic film. Let this marinate in the refrigerator for about 1 hour.

2. Puree the marinated ingredients in a blender until smooth and then season to taste with salt and pepper. Transfer the mixture to the refrigerator and let it sit for at least 1 more hour before serving.

3. Garnish with the avocado and basil.

CHILLED MELON SOUP WITH DICED PROSCIUTTO HAM

2 ripe cantaloupes
6 tablespoons port wine
Juice of 6 oranges (about 2 cups)
Water, as needed
Salt and pepper, to taste
2 thin slices Parma prosciutto ham,
    to garnish
1 small bunch fresh mint, to garnish

Serves 6

1. Clean the melons by removing the seeds with a large spoon and trimming away the skin.

2. Blend the meat of the melon with the port wine and orange juice in a food processor or blender. The thickness should be similar to tomato juice. If necessary, add a little water to thin the consistency. Season to taste with salt and pepper.

3. Let the soup chill in the refrigerator for a few hours before serving.

4. Finely julienne the prosciutto ham. Divide the cold soup among 6 bowls and then garnish each bowl with the prosciutto and a sprig of fresh mint.

SAUTÉED GULF SHRIMP SALAD

1 large Yukon gold potato, peeled and diced

2 heads romaine lettuce

¾ cup olive oil

2 cloves garlic, peeled

1 bunch Italian parsley (leaves only)

Salt and pepper, to taste

Milk, as needed

2 cups quinoa

1 teaspoon sweet chili sauce

½ cup duck stock or brown chicken stock

1 sheet 9-inch-diameter brick dough (or thin
    phyllo dough)*

Clarified butter, as needed

12 16/20-count shrimp, cleaned (heads and
    shells removed, deveined, tails on)**

Serves 4

**Brick dough is a thin, crepe-like dough that is similar
to phyllo dough but has more strength and does not
flake apart as phyllo does.*

***The number "16/20" refers to the size of the shrimp.
So 1 pound of 16/20-count shrimp should yield 16 to
20 individual shrimp.*

1. In a pot of boiling, salted water, cook the potato until it is tender throughout (7-8 minutes). Remove it from the water and reserve.

2. Using only the outside leaves of the romaine heads, cut the lettuce into slices to obtain 1 loosely packed cup. Set aside. Reserve the romaine hearts.

3. Heat ½ cup of the olive oil in a sauté pan over medium heat and then sear 1 of the garlic cloves on all sides. Add the cup of sliced lettuce, the cooked potato and the parsley. Season to taste with salt and pepper and sauté until the romaine has softened and is wilted (2-3 minutes).

4. Transfer the mixture to a blender and mix until smooth. If needed, you can add a little milk to the mixture to help it blend properly. (The consistency should be similar to a bisque-style soup.) Strain this coulis sauce through a chinois, discarding the solids, and then season it to taste with salt and pepper. Keep the coulis at room temperature.

5. Preheat oven to 400 degrees.

6. In another pot of boiling, salted water, cook the quinoa until it is tender (about 12 minutes or according to the instructions on the package). Strain the quinoa and then add the sweet chili sauce and stock, stirring well.

7. Brush some clarified butter on each side of the brick dough and cut it into 4 triangular pieces, in the same manner that you would slice a pizza. Roll each triangle-shaped dough piece around a cone mold. (If you do not have a cone mold, craft one using aluminum foil.) Bake the molded dough in the 400-degree oven for 2-3 minutes or until the dough is golden in color. (If you don't care to make cone-shaped dough, you can bake it into any shape you desire, as pictured; the baked dough is just a vessel in which to hold the quinoa.) Once the 4 cones have cooled, stuff each cone with some of the quinoa.

8. Add the remaining ¼ cup of olive oil to a nonstick pan over medium-high heat and sear the shrimp with the other clove of garlic for 2 minutes on each side. Remove the shrimp, add the reserved romaine hearts to the pan and cook for 1 minute. Don't overcook the hearts; you want them to retain their crunch.

9. Assemble the dish using 4 large plates or shallow bowls. Ladle some of the coulis into the middle of each plate or bowl. Set a quinoa-stuffed cone on top of the coulis and arrange some of the sautéed shrimp around the cone (or skewer them, as in the picture). Garnish with the cooked salad. Serve immediately.

THAI PAPAYA SALAD WITH SAUTÉED CALIFORNIA PRAWNS

1½ tablespoons butter

1 clove garlic, finely chopped

5 fresh California prawns or fresh jumbo
    shrimp, cleaned (heads and shells
    removed, deveined, tails on)

1 green papaya

2 ounces green beans (about ½ cup)

2 tablespoons palm sugar or granulated
    white sugar

1¾ ounces cherry tomatoes, sliced
    (about ¼ cup)

2 teaspoons chopped red chilies
    (or 1 teaspoon dried red chili flakes)

Juice of 1½ limes (about ¼ cup)

2 tablespoons Japanese fish sauce

¼ cup candied ginger, chopped*

3 cloves garlic, finely chopped and
    precooked**

⅛ cup peanuts, toasted

Fresh dill sprigs, to garnish

Fresh chives, chopped, to garnish

Serves 5

*Candied ginger comes in a jar and can be found in
most grocery stores. It has a more aggressive, bold
flavor than fresh ginger.*

**Precook the garlic by heating some olive oil in a
pan over medium heat and adding the chopped
garlic, cooking for 2-3 minutes. I prefer to add
cooked garlic to this dish because raw garlic can be
hard to digest.*

1. Warm the butter in a sauté pan over medium heat until it is just shy of pale brown. Add the uncooked garlic to the pan, continue to brown the butter and cook the garlic for 1 minute. Sauté the shrimp in the brown butter until they are opaque in the center (about 3 minutes). Season to taste with salt and pepper and keep warm.

2. Clean the papaya by removing the seeds, trimming away the skin and cutting the meat into rings.

3. Blanch the green beans in boiling, salted water for 2 minutes and then cool them in an ice bath to stop the cooking process. Remove.

4. Mix together all of the remaining ingredients (papaya, green beans, sugar, tomatoes, red chilies, lime juice, fish sauce, ginger, cooked garlic, green beans and peanuts). Let the salad sit at room temperature for at least 20 minutes to allow the flavors to marry.

5. Serve the salad in a large bowl with the warm shrimp on top. Garnish with the dill sprigs and chives.

COLORADO WARM GOAT CHEESE SALAD

1 red beet
1 golden beet
Sea salt, as needed
½ cup water
½ cup sugar
1 apple
1 4-ounce log goat cheese
Sugar, as needed (optional)
1 shallot, diced
1¾ teaspoons sherry vinegar
1 tablespoon grapeseed oil
Salt and pepper, to taste
2 lemons

Serves 4

1. Preheat oven to 350 degrees.

2. Sprinkle the beets with sea salt, wrap them in aluminum foil and then bake them in the 350-degree oven for 30-40 minutes (just like making a baked potato).

3. When the beets are tender enough to be easily punctured by the tip of a knife, cool, peel and cut them into a ¼ inch dice. Mix both beets together in a bowl and reserve.

4. In a medium saucepan, bring the sugar and the water to a boil, creating a syrup.

5. Peel and core the apple. Make ½ inch thick wheels, cutting across the apple. Add these slices to the syrup and let them simmer for 5 minutes. Remove the apple slices and reserve them on a cooking tray.

6. Divide the goat cheese into 4 1-ounce portions and then fashion each portion into a circle that is about the same size as the apple slices. Sprinkle some sugar over the goat cheese circles, lightly brulee them with a brulee torch and then allow to cool. (The brulee step is optional.) Place each 1-ounce portion on an apple slice and set aside.

7. Carefully fold the shallot, vinegar and grapeseed oil in with the reserved beets. Season to taste with salt and pepper.

8. Preheat oven to 300 degrees.

9. Make dried lemon zest by zesting the two lemons and then baking the zest in the 300-degree oven until it is dry. Portion the beet salad among 4 plates and then place one of the apple slices with goat cheese on top of each salad portion. Garnish the salad with the dried lemon zest.

DUCK CONFIT SALAD WITH POACHED EGG

DUCK CONFIT

1⅓ cups sugar

½ cup salt

¼ cup powdered cinnamon

2 tablespoons powdered cardamom

6 duck legs

2½ pounds duck fat

Pepper, to taste

3 shallots, chopped

2 tablespoons grapeseed oil

Water, as needed

Salt, as needed

White vinegar, as needed

6 eggs

3½ ounces frisée salad (about 6 cups)

RASPBERRY VINAIGRETTE

9 ounces (about 3 cups) fresh raspberries,
   crushed and strained to remove seeds

⅓ cup raspberry vinegar

¼ cup sugar

½ cup extra-virgin olive oil

Serves 6

1. In a small bowl, combine the sugar, salt, cinnamon and cardamom. Rub this into the duck legs and then place them on a sheet tray lined with plastic wrap. Press another sheet tray down on top of the wrapped duck legs and allow the meat to cure for 24 hours for optimum flavor.

2. After the duck legs have cured for 24 hours, wash them thoroughly and dry them with a cloth.

3. In a large Dutch oven, melt the duck fat over low heat and place the duck legs in the fat, making sure they are completely covered. Allow the duck to simmer very slowly in the duck fat. (This may take up to 3 hours.) The cooking process is complete when the meat on the duck legs can be easily pulled from the bone.

4. When the duck is cooked through, remove it from the fat and separate the meat from the bone. Discard the skin and bones and then chop the meat into small pieces. Place the meat in a bowl and toss it with the pepper, shallots and grapeseed oil. Reserve.

5. Fill a pan with 3 inches of water. Add a little salt and a touch of vinegar to the water and then bring it to a slight simmer. Carefully crack each egg into the water and remove them with a slotted spoon when they are done poaching (3-4 minutes). Place the eggs on a paper towel to drain.

6. While the eggs are draining, make the vinaigrette. Combine the raspberries, raspberry vinegar, sugar and olive oil in a bowl and then whisk until well incorporated. Set aside until time to serve.

7. Portion the duck meat among 6 plates. (I like to use a ring mold in order to shape the duck meat on the plate.) Place a poached egg on top of the duck and then add some of the frisée salad dressed with raspberry vinaigrette.

ASPARAGUS A LA FLAMANDE (FLEMISH-STYLE ASPARAGUS SALAD)

3 bunches jumbo white asparagus*
½ cup butter, melted
3 hard-boiled eggs, diced
1 cup Italian parsley, chopped
Salt and pepper, to taste
1 teaspoon grated nutmeg

Serves 4

I personally prefer white asparagus, but if you can't get the white variety or you prefer green asparagus, go for it. After all, you're the one eating it.

This sauce will remind you of a hollandaise sauce. It uses the same basic ingredients, but the technique given provides a much different texture; plus, it is far easier to make.

1. Peel the stem ends of the asparagus. Cook the spears in boiling, salted water for 5 minutes. Immediately submerge them in an ice-water bath to stop the cooking process. Dry the cooled spears and reserve. (You will reheat them right before serving.)

2. In a saucepan, melt the butter over medium heat, but do not allow it to brown.

3. Mix the diced eggs and chopped parsley into the butter, seasoning to taste with salt and pepper. Add the nutmeg.

4. To serve, reheat the asparagus, place it in the center of each plate and then pour the sauce over it.

ARTICHOKE SALAD

TOMATO CONFIT

2 medium-size tomatoes

4 cloves garlic

4 basil leaves

Extra-virgin olive oil, as needed

Salt and pepper, to taste

ARTICHOKES

6 fresh artichckes

Salt, as needed

ANCHOVY VINAIGRETTE

½ cup sherry vinegar

2 egg yolks

¼ cup Parmesan, finely grated

11 small anchovy filets

1⅓ cups vegetable oil

SALAD

1 pound baby arugula

½ cup black olives, sliced

Tomato confit (recipe at right)

Salt and pepper, to taste

Anchovy vinaigrette (recipe at right)

Salt and pepper, to taste

Shaved Parmesan, to garnish

Serves 6

1. Blanch the tomatoes for 10 seconds in boiling water (to make peeling them easier). Allow them to cool in ice water and then peel and discard the skin.

2. Slice each tomato in half and remove the seeds.

3. Place the sliced tomatoes, garlic and basil into a bowl and add enough olive oil to cover the ingredients. Season to taste with salt and pepper. Reserve. (It is best to prepare this the day before; it stays fresh for up to 1 week.)

4. Boil the artichokes in salted water for 30 minutes or until they are fork tender. Remove the leaves and reserve. Clean the artichoke heart and reserve.

5. To make the vinaigrette, add the sherry vinegar and egg yolks to a blender and mix well. Add the Parmesan and five of the anchovies and blend again. With the blender on, slowly add the vegetable oil until the vinaigrette reaches desired thickness. Reserve.

6. To assemble each salad, create a circular bed of the artichoke leaves on a plate. Place some of the baby arugula on top of the artichoke leaves. Cut each artichoke heart into 8 pieces and then mix it with a portion of the sliced olives and a slice of the tomato confit. Place this on top of the bed of artichoke leaves and arugula. Season to taste with salt and pepper and then pour some of the vinaigrette on top.

7. Finish the plates with the remaining anchovy filets and garnish with the Parmesan.

CRUSTY CRUST WITH GOAT CHEESE AND FRUIT COMPOTE, FRISÉE SALAD WITH ABBAYE DE LEFFE ORANGE VINAIGRETTE

PIZZA DOUGH

1 tablespoon plus 2¼ teaspoons milk

2 tablespoons plus 1½ teaspoons Abbaye
    de Leffe beer*

½ teaspoon yeast

½ cup flour

1 teaspoon olive oil

1 teaspoon salt

1 pinch herbes de Provence

FRUIT COMPOTE

2 quinces or apples

1 tablespoon sugar

VINAIGRETTE

½ cup fresh orange juice

¼ cup Abbaye de Leffe beer

¼ cup honey

⅛ cup apple cider vinegar

1½ cups extra-virgin olive oil

Salt and pepper, to taste

½ head baby frisée

PIZZA TOPPINGS

2 red bell peppers, roasted and peeled**

2 Roma tomatoes, peeled

3 zucchinis

1 16-ounce goat cheese log

Serves 4

*I like to use Leffe for its high yeast content and the
bold flavor that it adds to the crust.*

**To roast bell peppers, preheat broiler, halve each
pepper lengthwise and remove the stems, seeds and
membranes. Place the peppers on a baking sheet
skin side up. Broil the peppers for 10-12 minutes or
until blackened. Place them in a plastic, resealable
bag and seal, allowing them to stand for 10 minutes
(to make peeling them easier). After the peppers
have been in the bag for 10 minutes, the skin should
peel right off.*

1. Mix all of the pizza dough ingredients together using a mixer with the dough-hook attachment. Transfer to a bowl, cover with plastic wrap or a damp towel and let the dough rest for 2 hours in the refrigerator.

2. Preheat oven to 375 degrees.

3. On a floured work surface, roll out the dough to ⅛-inch thickness and then cut it into circles with a 3- or 4-inch ring mold to make 4 individual-size pizza crusts. Using a fork, poke small holes in the dough to keep it from rising.

4. Place the mini pizzas on a baking sheet and bake in the 375-degree oven for 4 minutes. Remove them from the oven and set aside. Reduce oven temperature to 350 degrees.

5. To make the fruit compote, peel the quinces or apples and cut them into small cubes. Place them in a saucepan over medium heat with the sugar and enough water to cover them. Cook until tender (about 20 minutes).

6. Transfer the fruit to a blender and then puree until you have the consistency of applesauce. Allow the puree to cool. Reserve.

7. To make the vinaigrette, pour the orange juice and beer into a saucepan over medium heat and reduce the liquid by half.

8. Pour the reduction into a blender and then add the honey and apple cider vinegar. Blend well. With the blender on, pour in the olive oil until the mixture is emulsified. Season to taste with salt and pepper. (Add a little water if the vinaigrette is too thick.)

9. Clean the baby frisée, place it in a salad bowl and then toss with some of the vinaigrette. Reserve. (The vinaigrette recipe will make more than you'll need; the unused portion will keep in the refrigerator for approximately 10 days.)

10. Slice the roasted peppers, tomatoes, zucchinis and goat cheese into little triangle shapes to fit the pizza form.

11. On the precooked mini pizzas, spread a layer of the fruit compote and then layer the bell peppers, tomatoes, zucchini and goat cheese over the compote.

12. Place the pizzas into the 350-degree oven for 3-4 minutes.

13. Serve the pizzas warm with salad on the side.

A SUMMER PIZZA FEUILLET

2 shallots, thinly sliced

½ cup vino santo (white vinegar from Italy)

Pepper mignonette, to taste*

Salt and pepper, to taste

2 carrots

⅛ cup cumin seed

2 tomatoes

1 tablespoon minced garlic plus 1 whole
   clove garlic

1 tablespoon dried thyme leaves

5 mini zucchinis, sliced

3 mini eggplants, sliced

2 yellow bell peppers, sliced

2 red bell peppers, sliced

½ cup olive oil

1 sprig fresh thyme

3 bay leaves

6 cups water

2 tablespoons honey

1 cup xeres (sherry) vinegar

2 cups chicken stock

4 artichoke hearts

2 cups milk

1 medium-size white onion, sliced

1 small turnip, halved and thinly sliced

1 tablespoon black peppercorns

1 tablespoon mustard seed

1 sheet puff pastry dough

2 eggs whites

Serves 6

Pepper mignonette is a classic blend of cracked Tellicherry black peppercorns, Muntok white peppercorns and coriander.

1. In a small pan over low heat, combine the shallots with the vino santo and then season to taste with pepper mignonette and salt. Slowly cook the mixture for 10-12 minutes, reducing to confit.

2. Cut the carrots into triangles, stir the pieces into the vino santo mixture and then add the cumin seeds. Reserve.

3. Boil the tomatoes in water for 10 seconds and then peel them. Cut the peeled tomatoes into quarters and then remove the seeds using a small spoon. In a bowl at room temperature, combine the tomatoes with the minced garlic and thyme leaves and then season to taste with salt and pepper. Allow the mixture to marinate for 15 minutes and then cut the tomato quarters into equal-sized triangles. Reserve.

4. Preheat oven to 350 degrees.

5. Place the zucchinis, eggplants, and yellow and red bell peppers in the 350-degree oven and then roast them for 5-7 minutes. Remove the vegetables and peel the peppers. (Reserve the zucchinis and eggplants.) In a small saucepan over low heat, combine the peppers, ½ cup olive, thyme sprig, garlic clove and bay leaves. Season to taste with salt and pepper and then slowly cook for 10-12 minutes. Drain the peppers and reserve.

6. In a large saucepan over high heat, combine the water, honey, xeres vinegar and chicken stock and then season to taste with salt and pepper. Bring the mixture to a boil. Cook the roasted zucchinis and eggplants in the boiling liquid for 5 minutes, then drain and peel them. Cut them into triangles and reserve.

7. In a saucepan over low heat, combine the artichokes and the milk and then season to taste with pepper. Allow the artichokes to simmer for 10 minutes and then remove them. (Discard the milk.) Reserve.

8. In a sauté pan, cook the onion in 2 tablespoons of the olive oil until they are translucent and then add the artichoke hearts.

9. Place the artichokes and onion in a blender with 3 tablespoons of the olive oil and mix until they reach a creamy consistency (resembling mayonnaise). Season to taste with salt and pepper and reserve.

10. In a saucepan of boiling water, submerge the turnips. Simmer them until they are tender (15-20 minutes). Remove the turnips from the water and then, when they are cool enough to handle, cut them into triangles. Reserve.

11. Preheat oven to 375 degrees.

12. With a round cutter, cut the dough into 2 circles measuring about 2½ inches in diameter and then brush them with the egg whites. Place the dough circles between two trays and cook them in the 375-degree oven for 4-5 minutes. Remove the pastry crusts and let them cool.

13. Spoon the artichoke-onion puree onto each pastry circle. Layer all of the vegetables over the puree-covered crust, alternating colors. Warm the pizzas in the 375-degree oven for 3 minutes just before serving.

SPICY PASTA WITH TOMATOES AND ARUGULA

2 teaspoons pine nuts

2 large cloves garlic

½ cup extra-virgin olive oil, plus more for
   sautéeing, as needed

2 cups tomatoes, seeded, peeled and
   coarsely chopped (about 1 pound
   whole tomatoes)

1 large jalapeño, seeded and chopped

Salt and pepper, to taste

1 pound fresh, small tagliatelle pasta

2 cups arugula (lightly packed)

Grated Parmesan, to taste

Serves 4

1. In a food processor, finely chop the pine nuts and garlic.

2. Transfer the pine nuts and garlic to a large nonstick skillet and lightly sauté them in a little olive oil. Allow them to cool and then add the tomatoes, ½ cup oil and jalapeño. Season the mixture to taste with salt and pepper. Let this stand for 1 hour at room temperature.

3. Cook the pasta in a large pot of boiling, salted water until it is just tender but still firm to the bite. Drain the pasta and reserve ¼ cup of the cooking liquid.

4. Add the pasta and the ¼ cup reserved cooking liquid to the tomato mixture. Stir over medium-high heat until the dish is heated through (about 4 minutes). Remove from heat, add the arugula and then toss to blend. Season to taste with salt and pepper and then add Parmesan to taste.

CHANTERELLE RAGOUT WITH ACORN SQUASH RAVIOLI

RAVIOLI DOUGH

1 pound all-purpose flour

1 egg

¼ cup extra-virgin olive oil

Salt and pepper, to taste

½ cup water, or as needed

2 eggs, yolks only

RAVIOLI FILLING

2 pounds acorn squash

1 cup orange juice

Honey, to taste

Star anise, ground, to taste

½ cup brown butter*

Salt and pepper, to taste

1 pinch ground nutmeg

RAGOUT

4 tablespoons butter

¾ pound chanterelle mushrooms (or other
   in-season mushroom), cleaned

¼ cup shallot, small-dice

3 cloves garlic, finely chopped

1 cup vegetable stock

3 sprigs fresh thyme, chopped, plus more
   sprigs to garnish

1 small bunch chives, chopped

Salt and pepper, to taste

Serves 6

*Using brown butter intensifies the flavor. To make
brown butter, simply heat butter in a pan until it
begins to brown.*

**If possible, allow the dough to rest overnight.*

†If you do not have a pasta machine, you can use a
rolling pin or wine bottle to sheet the dough to the
specified thickness.*

1. In the bowl of a mixer, combine the flour, egg yolks and olive oil and then season to taste with salt and pepper. Using the dough-hook attachment at low speed, mix the ingredients.

2. Slowly add water until the dough starts to come together (only add as much water as needed). Remove the dough from the bowl, wrap it in plastic wrap and place it in the refrigerator to rest for 1-2 hours.**

3. Preheat oven to 350 degrees.

4. To make the ravioli filling, cut the squash into quarters, remove the seeds and then place them in a baking dish, cut side up. Pour the orange juice over the squash and then drizzle with honey, to taste. Season to taste with the ground star anise. Roast the squash in the 350-degree oven until tender (about 45 minutes).

5. Using a spoon, scoop out the meat of the squash pieces into a blender or food processor. Blend the squash with the brown butter and the nutmeg and then season to taste with salt and pepper. Reserve.

6. Remove the ravioli dough from the refrigerator and use a pasta machine to sheet the dough. Start with the widest setting and continue sheeting with progressively more narrow settings until the dough is 1/16 inch thick (the instructions with your pasta machine can help walk you through the process).†

7. Place a sheet of dough on a work surface and cut it into rectangles 2 inches wide by 5 inches long. Each ravioli will require 2 2-inch-by-5-inch pieces of dough (one for the top side and one for the bottom side of the ravioli).

8. Place about 2-4 tablespoons of the ravioli filling on what will be the bottom piece of the ravioli, keeping the filling away from the perimeter edges of the dough.

9. Brush some egg yolk along the edges of the dough, around the filling, and then cover with the second (top) piece of ravioli dough. Press along the perimeter with your fingers or a fork to secure.

10. Cook the ravioli in boiling, salted water just until they rise to the top of the water (about 2 minutes). Cook them in small batches to prevent crowding. Use a slotted spoon to remove them from the boiling water and transfer them to a platter. Reserve.

11. To make the ragout, heat a sauté pan over high heat and then add the butter and mushrooms. Briefly sauté the mushrooms until they are tender and then add the shallot and garlic, cooking until they are tender (be sure not to burn the garlic). Add the vegetable stock, chopped thyme and chives to the ragout and then season to taste with salt and pepper.

12. To assemble the dish, serve the ravioli with the ragout in a large bowl or on a plate with broth on the bottom and top of the ravioli. Garnish with fresh thyme sprigs.

When I first immigrated to the United States from Belgium, I lived in South Carolina for a brief time. You might be surprised to read that I have been more impressed with the selection of seafood available to me here in Colorado than I was with the seafood in that coastal city. Because Colorado has no coasts, and because it is well-known for the quality of meat raised here, a lot of people come here with their minds made up not to eat seafood. But the fact is, with Denver having such a large airport that is centrally located between both of the major coasts, we can get fresh seafood flown in to Mirabelle from all over the place—and the quality is exceptional.

The seafood dishes we offer at Mirabelle, as well as the dishes highlighted in this chapter, include traditional preparations such as the Dover Sole Meuniere Mirabelle (recipe, page 82). But they also include more innovative preparations, particularly those that involve the use of beer, such as the Sauté of Monkfish on a Bed of Belgium Endives in Stella Artois Beer Sauce (recipe, page 84). Seafood is an important part of the menu at Mirabelle because I believe that eating it is a great way to feed yourself and is part of having a balanced diet. Unfortunately, though, I think a lot of people tend to neglect eating seafood at home. It tends to drop out of the normal cooking routine in many households, often because it can be difficult for the home cook to find really high-quality seafood at the local grocery store. You don't have to be a skilled chef to know when seafood is not fresh—either because of smell or appearance, subpar seafood jumps right out at you. And perhaps more than with any other ingredient, quality is extremely important when using seafood; if it's not fresh, the dish just isn't going to come out right. Accordingly, the most difficult part of preparing the recipes in this chapter might be putting in the effort to find the freshest, highest-quality seafood you can, which often means seeking out specialized fishmongers or even having it shipped in from other locations. After that, it's easy.

ASIAN INFUSED JUMBO SAUTÉED SCALLOPS

VEGETABLE FRY-FRY

1 zucchini

1 carrot, peeled

1 Yukon gold potato, peeled

1 red beet, peeled

Vegetable oil, for deep-frying

POLENTA WITH THYME FLOWERS

½ cup polenta

3 cups milk

½ cup fresh thyme flowers, chopped (just
    the flowers, no stems)

½ cup grated Parmesan

Salt and pepper, to taste

ASIAN SAUCE

3 tablespoons soy sauce

3 tablespoons rice wine vinegar

3 tablespoons balsamic vinegar

½ cup sesame oil

1 red bell pepper, finely julienned

½ cup fresh chives (cut into 2 inch lengths)

½ cup black sesame seeds

1 tablespoon pickled ginger, chopped*

¼ cup lemon zest

SEARED SCALLOPS

2 tablespoons clarified butter, or
    as needed

12 jumbo scallops (U-10)**

1 clove garlic, halved

Salt and pepper, to taste

Serves 4

**Also known as sushi ginger, pickled ginger is
available at most grocery stores. It comes in a jar
and is usually found in the condiments section.*

***The term "U-10" refers to scallops that come 10
per pound.*

1. Using a mandoline, slice all of the fry-fry vegetables into fine julienne, keeping them separate.

2. Cook the vegetables in a 350-degree fryer (or deep-sided sauté pan with an inch or two of oil) until crispy. After frying, transfer them to a paper towel to absorb the excess oil. Reserve.

3. In a sauce pan, add the polenta and milk and then bring to a simmer, stirring frequently and cooking until the polenta is soft (about 15 minutes). Add the thyme and the Parmesan at the very end of the cooking process, along with salt and pepper, to taste.

4. Transfer the polenta to a shallow baking dish and let it cool in the refrigerator for 1 hour. Cut the cooled polenta into 1 inch by 3 inch rectangles and then place them back in the refrigerator.

5. To make the Asian sauce, mix all of the sauce ingredients together in a salad bowl. Set aside.

6. Place a tablespoon of the clarified butter into a smoking-hot sauté pan. Sear the scallops 6 at a time (to prevent overcrowding the pan) with half of the garlic clove (just to season the butter). Do not shake the pan; turn the scallops only once, cooking them 1-2 minutes per side. Season to taste with salt and pepper. Remove the cooked scallops from the pan and reserve.

7. Using the same pan, add another tablespoon of the clarified butter and then warm the polenta rectangles, browning the pieces on both sides.

8. To serve, place 2 pieces of the polenta in the middle of each plate and arrange the scallops on top. Drizzle some of the Asian sauce around the plate and garnish with the colorful vegetable fry-fry.

GRILLED LOBSTER FRICASSEE WITH ROASTED GARLIC BROTH

GREEN HERBAL CROISILLON

1 bunch Italian parsley (flowers, no stems)

1 bunch cilantro (flowers, no stems)

½ cup water

⅓ cup powdered sugar

3 egg whites

1 cup high-protein flour (or bread flour)

LOBSTER FRICASSEE WITH ROASTED GARLIC BROTH

4 pounds live lobster (3-4 lobsters)

3 potatoes, peeled and diced

Salt and pepper, to taste

Extra-virgin olive oil, as needed

1 shallot, diced

½ pound chanterelle mushrooms or
   mixed mushrooms

5 fresh asparagus spears, peeled and sliced
   into 2 inch strips

1 cup cauliflower, cut into small florets

2 cloves garlic, roasted*

1 cup chicken broth

1 cup butter

½ cup chopped Italian parsley

Serves 4

*Roast the garlic cloves with the skin on in a 400-degree oven for 15 minutes (or until the garlic is tender).

**The French term "croissillon" refers to a lattice pattern. I chose this pattern because I like the way it looks. Feel free to use any pattern that pleases you.

†If you don't have a steamer, boil the live lobsters in lightly salted water for 3 minutes per pound.

This is a wonderful dish that incorporates many different flavors. Serve it warm in a soup bowl.

1. Preheat oven to 375 degrees.

2. In a blender, combine the Italian parsley, cilantro and water and then blend well. Place the mixture in a large bowl and mix in the sugar and egg whites by hand.

3. Slowly add the flour until the dough is flexible. (Use more than 1 cup if needed.) Transfer the dough to a pastry bag, or fashion one using parchment paper, rolling the paper into a tight cone and inserting a piping tip in the end.

4. Butter a parchment-lined sheet pan or spray it with nonstick spray and then pipe the dough into lattice patterns onto the parchment. Bake them in the 375-degree oven until they develop a little color (3-4 minutes). Reserve.**

5. Steam the lobsters by bringing 1½ inches of water to a boil in the bottom of a steamer pot. Add the lobsters to a steamer basket and place them into the pot to steam for 15 minutes.†

6. In a pan of lightly salted, boiling water, add the potatoes and then cook for 4 minutes (or until they are fork tender). Drain and reserve the potatoes.

7. Preheat grill to medium heat.

8. Remove the lobster meat from the tails and claws. Season the lobster meat with a little extra-virgin olive oil and salt and pepper to taste, and then place it on the hot grill, cooking each side for a minute or two (or until it is warm in the middle). Reserve.

9. In a large, nonstick pan over medium heat, sauté the shallot, mushrooms, asparagus, cauliflower and roasted garlic until the vegetables start to soften (about 3 minutes).

10. Add the chicken broth and butter to the pan and bring the liquid to a boil, raising the heat as needed. (Once the butter is well incorporated, it will make a smooth sauce.)

11. Add the potatoes and lobster meat to the pan and season to taste with salt and pepper.

12. Serve the lobster and broth in a large bowl. Add the chopped parsley to the bowl just before serving and garnish with the green herbal croisillon.

LOBSTER, MANGO CHUTNEY, CONFIT GINGER AND VANILLA, PASSION FRUIT TUILE

PASSION FRUIT TUILE

3½ tablespoons melted butter

¾ cup powdered sugar

⅓ cup high-protein flour

2 tablespoons passion fruit puree

2 tablespoons orange juice

MANGO CHUTNEY

1 mango

½ shallot, peeled and finely diced

Butter, as needed

5 teaspoons pickled ginger, diced*

½ lime, zested (use a microplane)

Salt and pepper, to taste

Xeres (sherry) vinegar, to taste

Cilantro, chopped, to taste

LOBSTER

4 live lobsters

1 onion, sliced

1 carrot, chopped

½ stalk celery, chopped

¼ cup red chili pepper flakes

SAUCE

½ onion, peeled and chopped

2 tablespoons unsalted butter

½ vanilla bean, split lengthwise and scraped

½ teaspoon curry powder

1 teaspoon coriander seeds

Juice of 2 oranges

1 mango, peeled and diced

1 tablespoon plus two teaspoons
    ginger, grated

3 sprigs fresh cilantro

Juice of ½ lime

Serves 4

*Pickled ginger, also known as sushi ginger, is available at
most grocery stores. It comes in a jar.*

1. Preheat oven to 350 degrees.

2. In a mixing bowl, combine all of the passion fruit tuile ingredients.

3. On a small, parchment-lined sheet tray, use a spoon to form 4 circles of the mixture about 2 inches in diameter. Cook the circles in the 350-degree oven until they are golden in color (about 3 minutes). Let the tuiles cool to room temperature. Reserve.

4. Peel and dice the mango.

5. Sauté the shallot in butter over medium heat until it is translucent (about 1-2 minutes).

6. Stir in the pickled ginger and lime zest and then season to taste with salt and pepper.

7. Deglaze the pan with the xeres vinegar, add chopped cilantro to taste and then toss the ingredients together with the mango. Set the chutney aside.

8. In a large pot of boiling, salted water, add the lobsters, onion, carrot, celery and chili pepper, cooking the lobster for 5 minutes (or 3 minutes per pound).

9. Transfer the lobsters to an ice bath to stop the cooking and then remove the tail and claw meat. Reserve.

10. To make the sauce, cook the onion in unsalted butter, in a saucepan over medium heat, until it is soft. Add the vanilla bean, curry powder and coriander seeds.

11. Deglaze the pan with the orange juice. Add the mango, ginger, cilantro and lime juice. Stir together and transfer to a blender to puree until smooth. Strain the mixture and keep warm.

12. Lightly sauté the lobster meat to reheat it, then, on each plate, arrange the lobster tail sliced in two pieces. Garnish with the chutney and a piece of claw meat.

13. Add the passion fruit tuile as a garnish and finish the dish by pouring some of the sauce around the plate.

GRILLED TUNA WITH ROASTED VEGETABLES, BALSAMIC LEMON VINAIGRETTE

ROASTED VEGETABLES

2 pounds acorn squash, peeled and cut into ½-inch dice

1 pound brussels sprouts, halved

1 pound carrots, cut into ½-inch dice

6 creamer potatoes (such as small Yukon gold or red potatoes), cut into ½-inch dice

1 whole clove garlic

Extra-virgin olive oil, as needed

Salt and pepper, to taste

2 teaspoons fresh rosemary

VINAIGRETTE

¼ cup balsamic vinegar

2 teaspoons grated lemon peel

½ cup olive oil

Salt and pepper, to taste

GRILLED TUNA

6 6-ounce fresh tuna filets

Salt and pepper, to taste

Olive oil, as needed

Serves 6

1. Preheat oven to 450 degrees.

2. Place the acorn squash, brussels sprouts, carrots, potatoes and garlic in a roasting pan with a drizzle of olive oil and then season to taste with salt and pepper. Stir to coat the vegetables well and then add the rosemary.

3. Cover the pan with aluminum foil and place it in the 450-degree oven until all of the vegetables are cooked (10-15 minutes or until they are fork tender). Reserve.

4. Preheat grill to high heat and then oil the grates.

5. In a small saucepan over low heat, combine the vinegar, lemon peel and the olive oil and season to taste with salt and pepper. Warm the vinaigrette just a bit.

6. Season the fish to taste with salt and pepper and then rub it with oil. Grill the tuna for about 2 minutes per side (or until it is cooked through) and reserve in a warm place.

7. To serve, transfer a portion of the vegetables to each plate and then top them with the tuna and the warm vinaigrette.

COLORADO TROUT WITH LEMON JAM

TROUT

4 trout filets (2 fish)

1 egg

½ cup cream

Salt and pepper, to taste

Butter, as needed

LEMON JAM

3 lemons, peeled and quartered

1 lime, peeled and quartered

1 cup sugar

1 star anise

1 sprig thyme

½ cup water

AVOCADO MOUSSE

2 zucchinis

2 avocadoes, peeled and pitted

Juice of 1 lemon

1 teaspoon cumin powder

Salt and pepper, to taste

Serves 4

Mousseline is a sauce to which cream or egg whites have been added, giving it a light, fluffy consistency.

1. Clean the trout, removing the bones and the skin. Using a ring mold about 2 inches in diameter, cut 2 circles out of each filet. Reserve the circles.

2. Put the rest of the trout meat in a blender with the egg and cream and then season to taste with salt and pepper. Blend this together well to obtain a smooth mousseline. (Be careful not to over-blend or the cream will break.)*

3. Spoon the creamy trout mousseline onto 2 of the circular pieces of trout and then place the remaining 2 circles on top (like a sandwich). Place in the refrigerator.

4. In a casserole dish over medium-low heat, add the quartered lemons and lime, sugar, star anise, thyme and water and let the mixture slowly simmer for 25 minutes. Be sure that the liquid isn't drying up; if needed, add a little water to maintain a syrupy consistency. Strain the mixture through a chinois (or fine mesh strainer) and reserve it in a clean saucepan.

5. Using a mandoline, julienne the zucchinis. In boiling water, blanch the zucchini strings for about 2 seconds and then shock them in an ice-water bath.

6. Using a mixer, make an avocado mousse by combining the avocadoes, lemon juice and cumin and season to taste with salt and pepper.

7. In a sauté pan, cook the trout circle "sandwiches" in a little butter for 2 minutes on each side.

8. To serve, place some of the avocado mousse on a plate. Arrange the zucchini strings in a flower shape and then set the trout against the flower. Drip some of the lemon syrup around the plate to finish.

POTATO-CRUSTED ALASKAN HALIBUT WITH JULIENNE OF SNOW PEAS

4 5-ounce halibut filets

1 teaspoon Dijon mustard

6 small potatoes (organic creamers such as small Yukon gold or red potatoes preferred)

1 pound cleaned snow peas

1½ cups vegetable broth

Salt and pepper, to taste

1½ cups peeled, seeded and chopped tomato

3 tablespoons butter

Fresh herbs such as chopped chives or parsley, to garnish

Serves 4

1. Preheat oven to 425 degrees.

2. Lightly brush the halibut filets with the Dijon mustard.

3. Very thinly slice the potatoes using a mandoline and overlap them on top of each filet to form "scales." (The mustard will help the potatoes stick to the fish.)

4. In an oven-safe pan, sear the fish potato-side-down until it is golden brown in color. Flip the halibut and finish cooking it in the 425-degree oven (about 3-5 minutes).

5. While the halibut filets are cooking, blanch the snow peas in boiling, salted water for about 2 minutes. Remove the peas from the boiling water with a slotted spoon and immerse them in an ice bath to stop the cooking process. Remove the cooled peas, dry them and cut them into strips lengthwise.

6. Heat the vegetable broth in a pan over high heat, bringing it to boil, and then add the peas and season to taste with salt and pepper. Add the tomatoes to the pan and finish the sauce by adding butter, to taste. Let this boil for a few minutes to incorporate the butter.

7. To plate, ladle some of the beans and sauce into a soup bowl and place 1 of the halibut filets on top. Garnish the dish with the chopped fresh herbs.

HALIBUT WITH SALSA OF PEARS, CUCUMBER, CARROT AND PINOT NOIR REDUCTION

SALSA

1 cup good-quality pinot noir

1 cup brown sugar

1 cup sugar

1 vanilla bean, split and scraped

2 star anise

1 cinnamon stick

3 carrots

1 English cucumber*

2 Anjou pears

Unsalted butter, as needed

1 cup vegetable stock, or as needed

Salt and pepper, to taste

HALIBUT

6 6-ounce halibut filets

Salt and pepper, to taste

Extra-virgin olive oil, as needed

1 lightly packed cup baby arugula

Serves 6

*Substitute a garden-variety cucumber if an English cucumber is unavailable.

1. In a large pot over medium heat, reduce the pinot noir with both sugars, the vanilla bean, the star anise, the cinnamon stick and 1 of the carrots. Let this cook slowly until the liquid has reduced by two thirds. Remove it from the heat to let it cool and steep. Strain before serving.

2. Peel the cucumber, the 2 remaining carrots and the Anjou pears. Using a small, parisienne scoop (melon baller), scoop round ball shapes out of each of the vegetables. Discard the hollowed-out vegetables.

3. In a nonstick pan over low heat, slowly cook the carrot balls first with a touch of unsalted butter. After 1-2 minutes, add a little vegetable stock. Let the liquid evaporate for about 3 minutes and then add the pears and cucumbers to the pan, cooking for 2 more minutes. Season to taste with salt and pepper. Reserve.

4. Season the halibut filets to taste with salt and pepper. In a warm nonstick pan over medium-high heat, cook the seasoned halibut in a little olive oil until it is cooked through (2-3 minutes on each side). Let the fish rest for a few minutes in a warm place.

5. In the same pan, add a bit more olive oil and sauté the baby arugula for a few seconds.

6. On each plate, first arrange the arugula and then add the halibut. Pour some pinot noir reduction on top and then cover everything with the salsa.

DOVER SOLE MEUNIERE MIRABELLE

Vegetable oil, for frying

3 Yukon gold potatoes

Salt and pepper, to taste

2 tablespoons extra-virgin olive oil

2 cloves garlic, crushed

1½ pounds baby spinach

6 whole Dover sole

Pepper, to taste

¾ cup butter, or as needed

6 tablespoons clarified butter

Juice of 2 lemons

6 tablespoons chopped parsley

Serves 6

At the restaurant, I garnish this dish with seasonal vegetables and herbs like asparagus, carrots and fennel. It's up to you as to what vegetables you enjoy most and, of course, what happens to be in season where you live.

1. Preheat the vegetable oil in a fryer to 300 degrees to make potato chips. Thinly slice the potatoes using a mandoline. Making sure that the potatoes are completely dry, set them in a small fryer basket to form a shape like a cornice (U-shape).

2. Fry the potatoes in oil for 4 minutes. Remove them from the basket and transfer to a paper towel to absorb the excess oil. Turn the oil temperature up to 350 degrees and re-fry the potatoes for 5-7 minutes or until they are golden brown in color. Remove them from the basket once again, drain the excess oil and dust them lightly with salt.

3. In a nonstick pan over medium heat, add the olive oil and garlic. Cook the garlic just until it turns light brown in color and then add the baby spinach to the pan and sauté for 2 minutes. Season to taste with salt. Remove the spinach from the pan and reserve (keeping it warm until it is time to serve).

4. For each whole Dover sole, season both sides to taste with salt and pepper. Add 1 tablespoon of the butter and 1 tablespoon of the clarified butter to a preheated nonstick pan over medium-high heat. Cook the butter until it begins to brown. Once the butter has browned, add 1 whole Dover sole and cook it for 3-4 minutes on each side. While the fish is cooking in the pan, use a spoon to baste the fish in the butter from the pan. When the fish is colored and cooked, remove it to a cutting board. Use a spoon to carefully remove the filets from the bones. Set the filets back into the pan and add 1 tablespoon of the remaining butter (not clarified), the lemon juice and the chopped parsley. Season to taste with salt and pepper. Repeat for each fish.

5. To assemble the dish, place some of the crispy potatoes on a plate, top them with some of the sautéed spinach and then add the Dover sole filets. Drizzle everything with some of the butter and parsley sauce.

SAUTÉ OF MONKFISH ON A BED OF BELGIAN ENDIVE IN STELLA ARTOIS BEER SAUCE

MONKFISH

2 pounds monkfish filets, cut into 1-inch strips

Salt and pepper, to taste

¼ cup all-purpose flour, or as needed

2 tablespoons unsalted butter

SAUCE

1 tablespoon unsalted butter

2 tablespoons minced shallots

1 cup Stella Artois beer

¾ cup heavy cream

Salt and pepper, to taste

ENDIVE

4 heads Belgian endive, sliced in half lengthwise

2 teaspoons sugar

1 tablespoon fresh lemon juice

1 tablespoon unsalted butter

CARROT

1 large carrot

Vegetable oil, for deep-frying

ASSEMBLY

Several sprigs chervil or 1 cup chopped parsley

Serves 4

1. Season the monkfish filets to taste with salt and pepper and then dust them with flour.

2. Melt 2 tablespoons of the butter in a large skillet over high heat. Add the fish and reduce the heat to medium. Sauté the fish until it is browned on both sides (about 5-7 minutes). Remove the fish from the skillet and keep it warm until it is time to serve.

3. Using the same pan (making sure it is dry), add the 1 tablespoon butter and melt it over medium-high heat. Add the shallot and sauté for 1 minute. Pour in the beer and cook, stirring for 1 minute. Add the cream and continue to cook to reduce the liquid by half. Season the sauce to taste with salt and pepper. Reserve.

4. Place the sliced endive in a bowl with the sugar and lemon juice and mix well.

5. Melt the 1 tablespoon butter in a second large skillet over medium heat. Add the endive, stirring frequently until it is slightly browned and caramelized.

6. Preheat oil in a deep fryer to 325 degrees. Peel the carrot and thinly slice it using a mandoline. Absorb any excess moisture with a paper towel. Carefully add the carrot chips to the hot oil and fry for 3-4 minutes. Transfer the chips to paper towels to absorb the excess oil and reserve. (The carrot chips can be made in advance.)

7. Just before serving, whisk the cream reduction using a small hand mixer to aerate the sauce and create a foam. To assemble the dish, place some of the caramelized endive on a plate and then top it with the monkfish and some of the foam. Finish by adding some fresh chervil (or chopped parsley) and carrot chips.

HOEGAARDEN-STEAMED SALMON WITH VEGETABLE TEMPURA AND SPICY TOMATO COULIS

SALMON

1 bottle Hoegaarden beer

6 5-ounce salmon filets

VEGETABLE TEMPURA

12 green beans

1 yellow squash

1 eggplant

1 onion

Vegetable oil, for deep-frying

1 bottle of very cold Hoegaarden beer

¼ cup chili powder

2 cups all-purpose flour

2 eggs (separate the yolks and whites)

1 pinch salt

TOMATO COULIS

4 whole tomatoes, chopped

½ onion, chopped

1 clove garlic, chopped

1 cup chicken or vegetable stock

Serves 6

The coriander and orange peel flavors in the Hoegaarden beer impart an amazing undertone to the steamed salmon. I am fond of this version of tempura. For me, it is lighter and more flavorful than the traditional ice-and-flour technique.

1. In a large sauté pan, add the bottle of beer and turn the heat on to high. Once the beer is boiling, add the fish, cover and drop the temperature down to medium heat. Keep the temperature of the pan the same throughout the cooking process. (If the beer comes back to a boil, the pan is too hot and needs to be turned down.) Allow the fish to steam with the pan covered for 6 minutes before checking it. The salmon should be cooked through but still moist inside.

2. While the fish is steaming, slice all of the tempura vegetables except the green beans into long strips (so that they are about the same size and shape as the green beans).

3. Preheat the oil in a deep fryer to 375 degrees. Make the tempura batter in a large mixing bowl by combining ¼ cup of the cold Hoegaarden beer with the chili powder and then slowly adding in the flour and 2 egg yolks.

4. In a separate bowl, whisk the 2 egg whites with the pinch of salt until they become stiff and hold peaks. Gently fold the egg whites into the tempura batter with a spatula. Dip the sliced vegetables into the tempura batter and then fry them in the hot oil until they turn golden brown in color. Transfer the tempura-fried vegetables to paper towels to absorb the excess oil and reserve.

5. Mix all the coulis ingredients together and cook them for 5 minutes in a saucepan over medium-high heat. Blend them in a blender until the coulis is smooth. Return the mixture to the saucepan and keep warm.

6. Place 1 salmon filet on each plate or bamboo steamer (optional) and arrange the vegetable tempura next to each filet. Ladle the tomato coulis into 6 small dishes and place a dish on each plate or steamer.

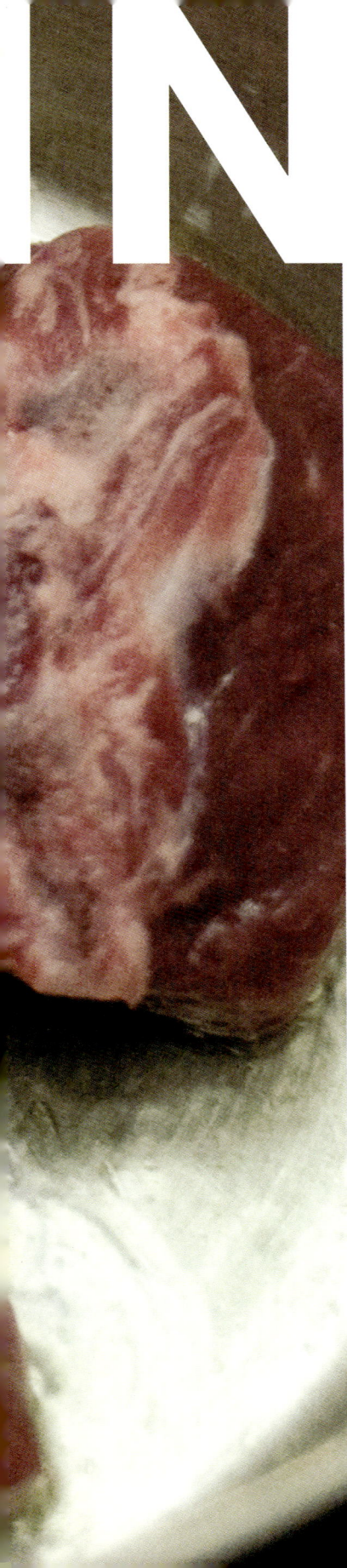

Colorado is a great state for finding local meat. While we have to fly in our seafood from remote locations, at Mirabelle we can find much of our meat right here in our own backyard. We always take the extra step of finding local meat producers who raise the finest-quality products, and that's what a lot of diners expect when they go out to eat in a ski-resort town like Beaver Creek. In the same way that spending time on the coast gets people thinking about seafood, the big open spaces and rustic ambiance of Colorado seem to put people in the mood for a nice piece of meat.

I think of meat as a comfort food, and I generally approach my preparations in an earthier way with more generous portions, as opposed to seafood preparations, which are often more elegant. As with much of the food at Mirabelle, our meat preparations range from traditional, as with the Colorado Rack of Lamb "Grand Daddy Style" with Garlic Mashed Potatoes (recipe, page 104), to more adventurous applications such as the Duck Breast with Wine-Poached Pears in Red Wine and Milk-Poached Celery Root Mousseline, Honey Soy Sauce (recipe, page 90). What they all share in common, though, is that if we're going to use a nice piece of meat, we want it to be the star of the plate. Even if I am marinating it with beer or using some other creative technique, I want the meat to be the main focus of the dish. I think you'll find throughout the book that at Mirabelle, whether we're highlighting the protein or some other ingredient, we like to take a clean, accessible approach to the food we make.

DUCK BREAST WITH WINE-POACHED PEARS IN RED WINE AND MILK-POACHED CELERY ROOT MOUSSELINE

DUCK BREAST AND PEARS

¼ cup milk

Salt, to taste

1 celery root, peeled and diced

Pepper, to taste

1 pinch ground nutmeg

About 1 teaspoon unsalted butter

½ bottle (375 ml.) good-quality red wine

2 cups sugar

1 vanilla bean

1 stick cinnamon

4 small pears, peeled

4 duck breasts (about 6-8 ounces each)

SAUCE

1 teaspoon butter

½ apple, diced

1 shallot, diced

3 tablespoons soy sauce

1 tablespoon honey

⅔ cup duck stock

PEAR CHIPS

1 pear, thinly sliced

2 cups water

2 cups sugar

Powdered sugar, as needed

Serves 4

*Mousseline is a sauce to which cream or egg whites have been added, giving it a light, fluffy consistency.

1. In a large casserole dish over high heat, combine the milk, a touch of salt and the celery root. Bring the milk to a boil and cook the celery root until it is cooked and tender (about 10 minutes).

2. Drain the celery root, place it in a blender and then puree. Season the puree to taste with salt and pepper and a pinch of ground nutmeg, and then add the unsalted butter. Blend everything together and place the celery root mousseline back into the casserole dish. Keep warm.*

3. In a saucepan, add the wine, sugar, vanilla bean and cinnamon stick. Add the pears and then poach them in the red wine reduction until they are cooked through (about 15 minutes). Reserve.

4. Season the duck breasts to taste with salt and pepper. In a nonstick pan over medium heat, cook the duck breasts for about 3 minutes on each side. Let the meat rest a few minutes before slicing.

5. Slice the cooked pears lengthwise into halves and, using a pomme parisienne (melon baller), hollow out the core of the pears and stuff with the celery root mousseline. Reserve.

6. To make the sauce, in a saucepan over medium heat, add the butter and cook the apple and shallot for 3-4 minutes. Deglaze the pan with the soy sauce and then stir in the honey, cooking until the liquid has reduced by half.

7. Add the duck stock to the pan and reduce to a syrupy consistency. Reserve.

8. Preheat oven to 150 degrees.

9. To make the pear chips, thinly slice the pear using a mandoline. In a saucepan over high heat, add the water and sugar and bring the liquid to a boil. (The sugar should be completely dissolved, creating a syrup.) Add the pear slices to the syrup and poach for a few seconds. Remove the pears from the syrup and set the slices in a nonstick pan. Dust the slices with powdered sugar and bake them in the 150-degree oven for 2 hours or until they are dry.

10. Set each duck breast slice on a plate with a stuffed poached pear on the side. Pour some of the sauce on top and finish with a few of the pear chips.

DUCK WITH BUTTERNUT SQUASH AND SOY SAUCE REDUCTION

4 small butternut squash

1 shallot, chopped

6 tablespoons honey

1 cup water

Salt and pepper, to taste

½ cup butter, plus more as needed

2 carrots, peeled

1 cup vegetable stock

Lavender, to taste

4 duck breasts

Vegetable oil, for sautéing

2 tablespoons soy sauce

2 tablespoons white soy sauce*

4 heads bok choy

Sea salt, as needed

Serves 4

*White soy sauce is clearer, thinner and saltier than dark (regular) soy sauce. If you have trouble finding white soy sauce, substitute with the dark variety.

**Quenelle typically refers to a dumpling formed into an oval shape using two spoons. While we're not making a dumpling, it's the oval quenelle shape that we're looking for in this dish.

1. Preheat oven to 350 degrees.

2. Cut each butternut squash into 4 pieces and place the pieces skin-side-up in a roasting pan along with the shallot, 4 tablespoons of the honey and water. Season to taste with salt and pepper. Place aluminum foil over the top of the pan and roast the squash in the 350-degree oven for 45 minutes. Remove the squash and leave the oven on at 350 degrees.

3. Remove the squash meat from the skins and put the meat in a blender. Add the butter and blend until the mixture is smooth. Reserve and keep warm.

4. With a pomme parisienne (melon baller), scoop out balls from the peeled carrots. In a saucepan over low heat, combine the carrots, the remaining 2 tablespoons honey and the vegetable stock. Season to taste with salt, pepper and lavender and then cook the carrots for 15 minutes. Reserve.

5. In a hot sauté pan over medium-high heat, sear the duck breasts in a little vegetable oil skin-side-down for a few minutes to slightly melt the skin and create a thin crust. Turn the breasts skin-side-up and finish cooking them in the 350-degree oven for 3 or 4 minutes, depending on the thickness of the duck breast. After allowing the meat to rest for a few minutes, reserve and keep it warm.

6. In a small saucepan add the soy sauce and reduce by half.

7. Slice the bok choy into quarters and then cook them in boiling water with a touch of sea salt for 4-5 minutes. Drain the water and shock the bok choy in an ice bath. (Blanching like this preserves the nice green color of the vegetable and cooks it al dente to retain some crunch.) Remove the bok choy from the ice bath and drain. Over low heat, warm the bok choy with a little butter, seasoning to taste with salt and pepper.

8. Place a quenelle** of butternut squash puree (or several, if you like) on each plate. Place 1 of the cooked bok choy heads (4 quarters) on each plate. Thinly slice the duck breast and set the slices on top of the bok choy. Add some balls of carrots to the plate and finish with some of the soy sauce reduction.

HERB PARMESAN-CRUSTED ELK TENDERLOIN WITH CREAM-POACHED SALSIFY, "RED" YUKON GOLD POTATOES AND PORT WINE REDUCTION

1 red beet

Salt, to taste

2½ pounds Yukon gold potatoes

4 salsify roots

2 cups water

½ cup all-purpose flour

Juice of 1 lemon

2 tablespoons heavy cream

Salt and pepper, to taste

Freshly ground nutmeg, to taste

4 tablespoons brown butter, plus more
   butter as needed*

6 elk tenderloin filets (about 6-7
   ounces each)

1 cup grated Parmesan cheese

½ cup chopped parsley

6 baby carrots, peeled

1 shallot, peeled and chopped

1 cup port wine

1 cup veal stock

12 green asparagus, stem ends peeled

½ carrot, chopped

Serves 6

To make brown butter, start with regular salted butter cut into pats. Add the pats to a saucepan over medium heat. While stirring, let the butter cook until it starts to develop a brown color and a nutty smell.

In this recipe, the red beet broth dyes the potato red, which provides a nice visual complement to the elk filets. Sometimes I like to add a fun salsify root garnish by thinly slicing some salsify with a mandoline, blanching it in simple syrup until it is tender and then drying it in a 200-degree oven for about an hour.

1. Cook the red beet in boiling water with a pinch of salt until the water is bright red. Remove the beet and strain the water into another saucepan, reserving the broth.

2. Peel and cut the potatoes into 6 block shapes of approximately 1 inch by 2 inches by 3 inches in size. Place the potatoes in the beet broth and bring to a simmer, cooking until the potatoes are cooked through but still firm (about 6-7 minutes).

3. Peel the salsify roots and slice them into 4-inch long pieces. In a medium-size saucepan, add the water, flour and lemon juice and mix well. Bring this mixture to a boil and add the salsify root, cooking the pieces for about 6-7 minutes. Turn off the heat and reserve them in the broth.

4. In a small saucepan over medium heat, add the cream, season to taste with salt, pepper and freshly ground nutmeg, and then reduce the liquid by half. After the liquid is reduced, remove the salsify root pieces from the broth and add them to the cream. Remove the pan from the heat and let stand until ready to serve.

5. Preheat oven to 375 degrees.

6. Add the brown butter to a nonstick pan over medium-high heat and cook the elk tenderloin filets for 2 minutes on each side. Transfer the meat to an oven-safe pan or dish to finish cooking. Before placing the meat into the oven, cover the top of each filet with Parmesan and chopped parsley. About 3-5 minutes in the oven will cook the meat to medium-rare and provide a cheesy herb crust.

7. Wipe the brown butter out of the pan and add the carrots, shallot, port wine and veal stock and then reduce the liquid by half or until it reaches a nice sauce consistency.

8. Cook the asparagus and chopped carrot in boiling water for 2 minutes. Remove the vegetables from the water, drain and add them to a warm pan with a little butter. Season to taste with salt and pepper.

9. On each plate, place some of the salsify pieces and add a potato on top. Set the elk slices on the potato. Garnish with the asparagus and chopped carrot.

FRESH FREE-RANGE CHICKEN WITH VEGETABLE GATEAU, TOMATO AND BELL PEPPER JUS

CHICKEN AND VEGETABLES

4 large yellow onions

Extra-virgin olive oil, as needed

Sea salt, to taste

3 peeled potatoes, small dice

2 zucchinis, small dice

2 yellow squash, small dice

2 red bell peppers, small dice

1 cup mushrooms, small dice

1 clove garlic

Salt and pepper, to taste

4 free-range chicken breasts

Sesame seeds, to garnish

TOMATO AND BELL PEPPER JUS

½ cup extra-virgin olive oil

1 shallot, chopped

1 clove garlic, peeled

1 red bell pepper, diced

1 yellow bell pepper, diced

1 ripe tomato, diced

Salt and pepper, to taste

1 cup vegetable stock

Serves 4

*To make the Parmesan and black olive crust, mix together ½ cup grated Parmesan with ½ cup melted butter, a little less than ½ cup sliced black olives and ½ cup all-purpose flower. On a Silpat (or a baking sheet coated with cooking spray), spread the mixture out evenly and bake in a 350-degree oven for 20 minutes or until crispy.

1. Preheat oven to 375 degrees.

2. Place the whole onions in an oven-safe dish. Drizzle generously with olive oil and season to taste with sea salt. Roast the onions for 2 hours in the 375-degree oven. When the onions are cooked, remove the skins. Then remove the first 2 meaty layers to make a cup shape. Cut the rest of the onions into small dice.

3. Starting with the varieties that take the longest to cook, place the diced vegetables in a warm skillet with olive oil in this order, allowing a minute of cook time between each addition: potatoes, zucchinis and yellow squashes, red bell peppers, mushrooms, garlic and the cooked diced onions. Cook the vegetables for 3 more minutes and then season to taste with salt and pepper. Reserve.

4. Preheat grill to high heat.

5. Rub a little salt and pepper into the chicken breasts. Cook the breasts on the grill, turning them frequently to avoid burning. It will take about 15 minutes for the breasts to cook fully but still remain juicy in the middle. Set aside.

6. For the jus, use a saucepan to warm the olive oil over medium heat. Add the shallot, garlic, peppers and tomato and cook them slowly for about 1 minute. Season to taste with salt and pepper and then cover the vegetables with the vegetable stock. Cook for 5-6 minutes. Transfer the jus to a blender and blend until it is smooth. Season to taste and then strain through a chinois.

7. To serve, pour some bell pepper jus onto each plate and place the cooked vegetables in an onion cup in the center of the plate. Set a chicken breast next to the onion cup and pour more bell pepper jus over the chicken. Garnish with a crust of Parmesan and black olives.*

GRILLED BEEF TENDERLOIN WITH BRAISED ENDIVES AND POMMES GALETTE

4 8-ounce beef filets
Salt and pepper, to taste
1 cup red wine
2 shallots
2 teaspoons sugar
1 cup veal stock
Butter, as needed
4 Belgian endive heads
Water, as needed
5 creamer potatoes (such as small Yukon
   gold or red potatoes)
Olive oil, as needed

Serves 4

1. Preheat grill to medium high.

2. Season both sides of the beef filets to taste with salt and pepper and then grill them to desired doneness, turning once. Reserve.

3. In a saucepan over medium heat, cook the red wine, shallots and 1 teaspoon of the sugar until the liquid completely reduces. Add the veal stock and boil it for a few minutes. Reserve the sauce and keep warm.

4. In another saucepan over medium heat, add a spoonful of butter and the endives and cook them covered with a little bit of water to steam them. After 10 minutes, add the remaining 1 teaspoon sugar and then turn the heat up to medium-high to caramelize the endive. Reserve.

5. Preheat oven to 400 degrees.

6. For the pommes galette, thinly slice the potatoes using a mandoline. Line a sheet pan with parchment paper. Arrange the slices on the sheet pan, overlapping them slightly. Drizzle olive oil over the top and lay another sheet of parchment paper over the potatoes. Place another sheet pan on top of the paper. Place the tray of potatoes in the 400-degree and cook them until the slices are colored and cooked (4-5 minutes).

7. Remove the tray from the oven and set the potatoes on a paper towel to absorb the extra oil before serving. Cut with a knife a galette (a large rectangle, approximately 2 inches by 5 inches).

8. To serve, first place the endives on a plate, followed by the meat. Pour some of the red wine sauce on the meat. To garnish, put the pomme galette on top of the filet.

GRILLED FREE RANGE VEAL CHOP WITH BROCCOLI MOUSSELINE, MOREL SAUCE

BROCCOLI MOUSSELINE

5 Yukon gold potatoes, peeled and diced

2½ cups broccoli flowers

Salt and pepper, to taste

Ground nutmeg, to taste

½ cup mascarpone cheese

CARROTS, VEAL AND MOREL SAUCE

12 baby carrots

4 8-ounce free-range veal chops

1 shallot, diced

2 tablespoons unsalted butter, or as needed

¼ pound morel mushrooms

½ cup red wine

2 cups veal stock

Salt and pepper, to taste

Serves 4

*Mousseline is a sauce to which cream or egg whites have been added, giving it a light, fluffy consistency.

1. Place the diced potatoes in a pot of boiling, salted water and let them cook for 10 minutes. Add the broccoli flowers to the boiling water with the potatoes and let them cook together for 2 more minutes.

2. Strain the vegetables and then pass them through a food mill. Season to taste with salt, pepper and nutmeg. Mix in the mascarpone cheese and reserve the mousseline.*

3. Cook the baby carrots in boiling, salted water until they are tender and then set aside.

4. Preheat grill to medium-high heat and then grill the veal chops on both sides, turning them frequently to obtain medium-rare doneness.

5. While the chops are cooking, warm a saucepan over medium-low heat with the shallot and a little unsalted butter, cooking the shallot slowly for a few minutes. Add the mushrooms and red wine. Let the wine evaporate and then add the veal stock. Let the liquid reduce to sauce consistency (coats the back of a spoon). Finish the sauce with unsalted butter and season to taste with salt and pepper before serving.

6. Place each veal chop on top of a bed of broccoli mousseline. Arrange the baby carrots around the meat and pour the morel sauce over the dish.

ROASTED COLORADO RACK OF LAMB WITH ZUCCHINI AND ARTICHOKE BALLOTINE AND GARLIC EMULSION

4 ounces fresh thyme

4 ounces fresh tarragon

4 ounces fresh chervil

4 ounces panko bread crumbs

Extra-virgin olive oil, as needed

2 cloves garlic, peeled

4 3-bone racks of Colorado lamb (5-6
    ounces each), frenched

1 egg

3 zucchinis

6 artichoke hearts, cleaned and pre-cooked

1 cup brown butter*

Salt and pepper, to taste

1 large Yukon gold potato

Milk, as needed

Serves 4

To make brown butter, start with regular salted butter cut into pats. Add the pats to a saucepan over medium heat. While stirring, let the butter cook until it starts to develop a brown color and a nutty smell.

1. Trim the stems from the thyme, tarragon and chervil. Using a food processor or blender, puree the herbs and the panko bread crumbs for 30 seconds and then spread them on a plate. Set aside.

2. Over medium-high heat, add a drizzle of olive oil to a nonstick pan. Add the garlic cloves to the pan and then add the lamb, searing on all sides. Remove from heat and allow the meat to cool.

3. When the lamb is cool, whisk the egg and pour it onto a plate. Roll the meat in the egg to coat it and apply the herb mixture all over the lamb racks. Set them aside.

4. Slice the zucchinis on a mandoline or by hand to about ¼-inch thickness. In a sauté pan over medium-low heat, slowly cook the zucchinis in olive oil until they are soft and flexible (this will only take a few seconds, since the zucchini is sliced thinly). Place the softened zucchinis on a paper towel to absorb the excess oil. Use a ring mold about 1 inch in diameter to create a cup shape using the zucchini slices. (Make 4 cups.)

5. In a blender, mix the artichoke hearts with 2 tablespoons of the brown butter; season to taste with salt and pepper and then blend until smooth (about 1 minute). Fill each zucchini cup with the artichoke mixture to create the ballotines.

6. Preheat oven to 375 degrees.

7. Peel and slice the potato. Lay the slices in a baking dish and add enough milk to cover the potato. Add the garlic cloves (used when searing the lamb) and a pinch of salt. Cover the dish with foil and cook in the 375-degree oven until the potatoes are tender (about 15 minutes). Remove the potatoes and garlic from the dish (reserving the milk) and place them in a blender with 2 tablespoons extra-virgin olive oil. Mix for 20 seconds to make a garlic-potato mousseline. The resulting mixture should have a sauce-like consistency. If it is too thick, add some of the milk from the baking dish and blend until the correct consistency is achieved. Reserve the remaining milk (for making the foam used in plating the dish).

8. Place the lamb in a roasting pan and finish cooking in the 375-degree oven (8-10 minutes or until it is done to your liking). Remove the meat from the oven and allow it to rest in a warm place. Reduce the oven temperature to 300 degrees. In the same roasting pan used for the lamb, warm the zucchini-artichoke ballotines for about 5-6 minutes or until they are warm in the middle.

9. Add the reserved milk to a blender and mix on high speed just for 1-2 seconds to create a foam. The milk should be nice and cool by the time you add it to the blender. (If it is too hot, it will not form the foam.)

10. On a large plate, set 1 of the zucchini-artichoke ballotines in the middle, add some of the potato mousseline with a spoon on the bottom of the plate and then add the lamb. Drizzle some of the lamb jus over the plate to finish.

COLORADO RACK OF LAMB "GRAND DADDY STYLE" WITH GARLIC MASHED POTATOES

4 whole cloves garlic, plus 1 clove
    chopped

Milk, as needed

2 racks Colorado lamb (8 bones each)

½ cup extra-virgin olive oil, or as needed

Salt and pepper, to taste

10 baby fingerling potatoes, peeled

1 pinch sea salt

1 pinch nutmeg

Finely chopped chives, to taste

13 sprigs fresh rosemary, leaves finely
    chopped

½ cup white wine

1 fresh tomato, chopped

1 tablespoon unsalted butter

1 pound baby spinach

Serves 6

Our regular guests often request this classic Mirabelle dish.

1. Peel the 4 whole cloves garlic and set them in a small pan. Cover them with milk and cook slowly over medium heat for 9 minutes. Drain the excess milk through a strainer and place the garlic in a food processor, mixing until smooth. (Reserve the garlic puree in a small container; it will keep in the refrigerator for several days.)

2. In a hot sauté pan, sear the lamb with a drizzle of olive oil. Sear the lamb until it has a nice brown crust. Remove the meat from the pan and season to taste with salt and pepper. Reserve.

3. For the potato mash, place the peeled fingerling potatoes in a large saucepan over medium-high heat with enough water to cover the potatoes and add a pinch of sea salt. Cook the potatoes until they are tender and then pass them through a food mill. Season to taste with olive oil, some of the garlic puree, salt, pepper and a touch of fresh nutmeg. Add the finely chopped chives at the end.

4. Set aside about 1 teaspoon of the chopped rosemary and place the rest on a plate. Cover the lamb in garlic puree and then roll it in the chopped rosemary to coat.

5. Place the lamb in a baking dish and finish cooking it under the broiler to get a light crust from the rosemary and garlic (about 4-5 minutes). Reserve the drippings. Allow the lamb to rest in a warm place.

6. In a saucepan over medium heat, add the lamb drippings, white wine, the clove of chopped garlic, tomato and reserved 1 teaspoon rosemary leaves; reduce for 20 minutes or until you achieve a sauce-like consistency. Add the unsalted butter to finish the sauce.

7. In a sauté pan with a drizzle of olive oil, sauté the baby spinach with freshly ground pepper.

8. On a plate, arrange the spinach and mash in a ring. Add the lamb and drizzle the sauce over it.

BUFFALO TENDERLOIN, MARINATED WITH STELLA BEER, BELGIAN SALSIFY AND POMMES GALETTE

1½ pounds buffalo tenderloin, trimmed and
    portioned into 6-ounce steaks

Salt and pepper, to taste

Butter, as needed

1 celery root, peeled and chopped

1 fennel bulb, chopped

2 Anjou pears, peeled and diced

1 cup pineapple chunks

1 cup honey

1 tablespoon balsamic vinegar

2 onions, peeled and chopped

1 leek, white parts only, chopped

1 carrot, peeled and diced

1¼ cups red wine

1 bottle Stella Artois beer

2 Yukon gold potatoes

Extra-virgin olive oil, as needed

2 cups water

1 tablespoon all-purpose flour

Juice of 1 lemon wedge

5 sticks salsify (2½ sliced, 2½ whole)

2 tablespoons brown butter*

1¼ cups veal stock

Serves 4

To make brown butter, start with regular salted butter cut into pats. Add the pats to a saucepan over medium heat. While stirring, let the butter cook until it starts to develop a brown color and a nutty smell.

1. One day before serving, season the buffalo steaks to taste with salt and pepper and then sear the meat on all sides in butter over medium-high heat until a light brown crust forms.

2. In a bowl large enough to accommodate the meat, combine the celery root, fennel, pears, pineapple, honey, balsamic vinegar, onions, leek, carrot, red wine and Stella. Set the meat in the marinade and refrigerate it for 24 hours.

3. Using a cutter 1 inch in diameter, cut down each potato vertically to create cylinders. With a mandoline, cut the cylinders into thin slices. On parchment paper, arrange the potato disks so that they overlap and create a larger circle 4 inches in diameter. Repeat to make 4 of these.

4. Preheat oven to 375 degrees.

5. In a nonstick pan over medium-high heat, add a drizzle of olive oil and cook each of the potato circles on both sides for 2 minutes. Reserve until time to serve.

6. In a medium-size saucepan, add the water, flour and lemon juice and mix well. Bring this mixture to a boil and add the salsify root, cooking the pieces for about 6-7 minutes. Remove them from the water and sear in a nonstick pan with beurre noisette (brown butter). Reserve until you are ready to plate.

7. Transfer the meat from the marinade to an oven-safe pan. In a saucepan over medium heat, add the marinade and the veal stock and reduce to one fourth of its volume. Strain through a fine-mesh strainer to obtain a smooth sauce and reserve.

8. Put the buffalo in the 375-degree oven to finish cooking it to medium-rare doneness (about 4 minutes).

9. Place portions of the salsifies and buffalo steaks on each plate and cover them with the sauce. Add a potato galette to each plate.

STELLA ARTOIS-MARINATED FLANK STEAK

MARINATED FLANK STEAK

¼ cup soy sauce

1 tablespoon sesame oil

3 large cloves garlic, chopped

2 teaspoons Dijon mustard

2 teaspoons Worcestershire sauce

1 teaspoon ground black pepper

½ cup Stella Artois beer

6 8-ounce portions flank steak

LEFFE VEGETABLE TEMPURA

Vegetable oil, for frying

8 ounces Leffe beer, ice cold (put in freezer, or use 7 ounces beer and 2 ice cubes)

1 egg yolk

1 teaspoon salt, plus more to taste

3 tablespoons all-purpose flour or potato flour, plus more all-purpose flour for dredging the vegetables

¼ pound asparagus tips (about 3 inches long)

¼ pound carrots, cut into 3-by-½-inch sticks (batonette)

¼ pound green beans

¼ pound zucchini, cut into 3-by-½-inch sticks (batonette)

¼ pound red bell pepper, cut into 3-by-½-inch sticks (batonette)

Serves 6

1. One day prior to serving, combine the soy sauce, sesame oil, garlic, mustard, Worcestershire sauce, black pepper and Stella Artois in a bowl large enough to hold the steak. Submerge the steak in the marinade mixture and cover it with plastic wrap. Chill for a full day, turning the steaks occasionally.

2. On the day you are serving the steaks, preheat grill to medium-high.

3. Grill the beef on the medium-high grill until it reaches medium-rare doneness (5-6 minutes per side).

4. Transfer the steak to a carving board and let it rest 15-20 minutes.

5. While the steak is resting, bring the vegetable oil to 350 degrees in a deep-fryer.

6. Mix the Leffe, ice (if using), egg yolk and salt until just combined. Evenly sprinkle the 3 tablespoons flour over the mixture.

7. Working in batches, dip the vegetables into the batter and then drop them into the deep-fryer until they are lightly golden in color (about 2 minutes). Transfer them to paper towels to absorb excess oil. Season to taste with salt.

8. Thinly slice the steaks across the grain. Arrange them on a platter and spoon any accumulated juices over the meat. Serve with the Leffe vegetable tempura.

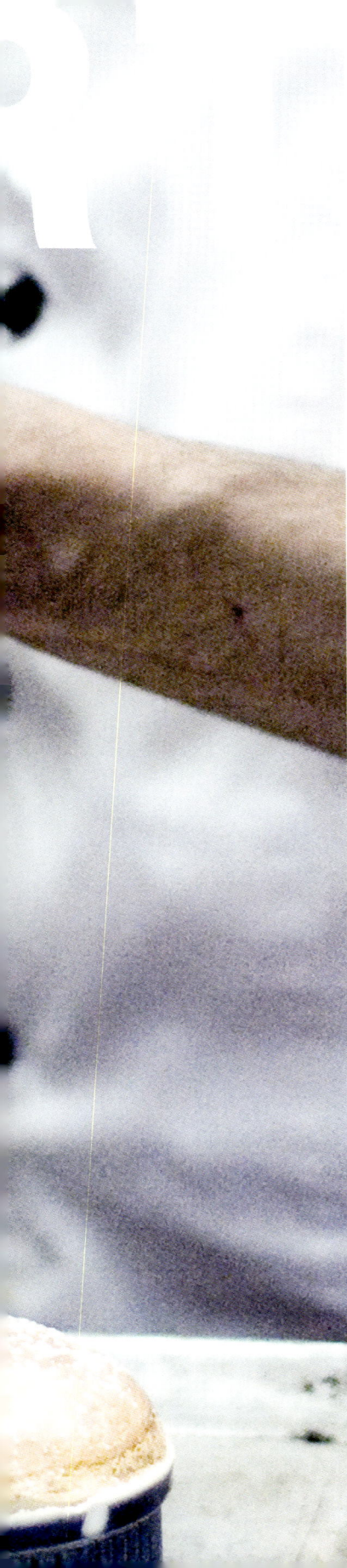

We take desserts very seriously at Mirabelle, because they bring the finishing touch to a meal. When I talk to a lot of people who have eaten here, even though they might have ordered five or six courses, the only thing they might remember is the dessert—not because they didn't enjoy the earlier courses, but because the dessert was their last impression.

We have about seven desserts on the menu at the restaurant at any given time, and they generally fall into two broad categories. Some are what I call the "classic" Mirabelle desserts, those in our portfolio that people request over and over again and that we can make for them at any time, such as the "Our Friend Maria's" Lemon Meringue Tart (recipe, page 113) and the Grand Marnier Soufflé (recipe, page 120). We round out the dessert list with dishes that change daily, allowing the pastry chef to be a little more creative with bringing in seasonal ingredients and new variations. One thing that applies to every recipe in this chapter, though, is that preparing a dessert is more like chemistry than any other type of dish. It is very important to respect the measurements of ingredients to make sure everything comes out right. With a lot of the recipes elsewhere in this book, you can alter a few things as you go along; but in pastry, if you change things such as the proportion of eggs to flour, you will end up with an issue in the final result.

I anticipate that the most frequently visited section of this book might be the 11 cookie recipes at the end of this chapter (page 154). I included them because I can imagine so many situations in which these simple recipes would be useful. Say you're having friends over for coffee, and you don't want to do bother with an elaborate dessert preparation. Or maybe you need to brings some sweets to a pitch-in function at your child's school. Or maybe you just want a delicious afternoon snack.

"OUR FRIEND MARIA'S" LEMON MERINGUE TART

SUGAR DOUGH

1½ cups all-purpose flour

½ teaspoon salt

½ cup sugar

1 egg

7 tablespoons butter, softened

LEMON CREAM

4 lemons, zest only

1 cup sugar

10¾ tablespoons butter

4 eggs

3 tablespoons cream

LEMON SORBET

1 cup freshly squeezed Meyer lemon juice

2½ cups granulated sugar

4 cups water

2½ tablespoons glucose sugar (or corn syrup)

SWISS MERINGUE

1½ cups granulated sugar

1 cup egg whites

Serves 8

1. To make the sugar dough, place the flour in a medium mixing bowl.

2. In a separate container, add the salt, sugar and egg and then, using a handheld mixer with the whisk attachment, combine the ingredients until the sugar has dissolved.

3. Add the softened butter to the sugar mixture and then whisk briefly, (about 1 minute).

4. Make a well in the center of the flour and pour the sugar mixture into the well. Use a spatula to mix the sugar mixture into the flour. Cover the bowl and set the dough in the refrigerator to rest for 1½ hours.

5. Preheat oven to 350 degrees.

6. On a lightly floured work surface, roll the chilled dough out to ¼-inch thickness. Lay the dough across a 10-inch tart pan and press it down into the corners of the pan. Pierce the dough several times with the tines of a fork.

7. Bake the tart shell in the 350-degree oven for 15 minutes, or until the crust is golden brown in color. Remove the tart shell from the oven and reserve.

8. In a medium saucepan over medium-low heat, combine all of the lemon cream ingredients. Whisk them continuously until all of the ingredients are fully incorporated and reach a simmer. Cook at a low simmer for 2 minutes.

9. Place the lemon cream ingredients in a medium bowl and set them in the refrigerator to cool.

10. In a medium saucepan over medium-high heat, combine all of the lemon sorbet ingredients and cook them until they reach a boil.

11. Transfer the ingredients to an ice cream machine and follow the manufacturer's instructions. Place the sorbet in a freezer and reserve.

12. Set up a bain-marie (or water bath) by bringing a pot of water to a strong simmer and placing a stainless-steel bowl over the top of the pot. Add the sugar and egg whites to the bowl.

13. Slowly mix the ingredients until the sugar has melted, then whip vigorously with a whisk to "raise" the meringue. When the meringue reaches 131-140 degrees on a candy thermometer, remove from heat and continue whipping until the meringue cools. Reserve.

14. Preheat oven to 450 degrees.

15. In a small saucepan over low heat, warm the lemon cream, whisking constantly. Pour the warm lemon cream into the cooled tart crust.

16. Place the meringue in a pastry bag and pipe around the top of the lemon tart.

17. Bake the tart in the 450-degree oven for 2 minutes, or until brown in color. Use a kitchen torch to caramelize the top and serve with a scoop of the lemon sorbet.

PEAR TART "MOELLEUX"

PEAR CAKES

2 Anjou pears, peeled and sliced

4 tablespoons unsalted butter, softened

⅓ cup granulated sugar

2 eggs

1 cup all-purpose flour

2¾ teaspoons dry yeast

VANILLA CREAM

1 cup heavy cream

1 vanilla bean, split, seeds removed

½ cup granulated sugar

CANDIED PEARS

2 cups water

2 cups granulated sugar

20 balls of Anjou pear (scooped from the
   pear, using a parisienne scoop)

2 cups sauvignon blanc

Serves 4

To cook the pear balls without a water circulator, place them in a pan with the sauvignon blanc and simple syrup (recipe at right) and then cook them, covered, over low heat for about 20 minutes.

1. Preheat oven to 350 degrees.

2. In a medium mixing bowl, combine the pear slices, softened butter, sugar, eggs, flour and yeast and then stir the ingredients.

3. Pour the mixture into each of 4 3-inch silicone molds and bake the little cakes in the 350-degree oven for 10 minutes. Remove the pear cakes from the oven and set aside.

4. In a medium mixing bowl, combine the heavy cream, vanilla bean seeds and sugar and then whip the ingredients. Reserve the whipped cream in the refrigerator until ready to plate.

5. Preheat a water circulator (or slow cooker) to 135 degrees.*

6. For the candied pears, make simple syrup by slowly simmering the water and sugar in a pan for about 5 minutes. Remove from heat.

7. Place the pear balls, simple syrup and sauvignon blanc in a vacuum-seal bag and then seal the bag. Cook the pears in the 135-degree water circulator for 3 hours, or until it makes a candy.

8. To serve, place the candied pears on top of the pear cakes and top with the vanilla cream.

CRÈME BRÛLÉE

12 egg yolks

1 cup sugar

3 vanilla beans, split, seeds removed

1 cup milk

3 cups heavy cream

Turbinado sugar, to garnish*

Berries, to garnish

Fresh mint, to garnish

Serves 12

*Turbinado sugar is a coarse, raw sugar with a flavor that resembles molasses.

**To temper the egg mixture, add about half of the milk and cream a little at a time before combining the mixture with the remaining milk and cream mixture.

†To make a double water bath, set the forms in a hotel pan (or deep-sided baking sheet) and place the pan in the preheated oven, leaving the edge of the pan hanging slightly over the front of the oven rack (to keep from having to reach into the oven). Pour hot water into the pan until it is about ¾ full, being careful not to splash any water onto the brûlées. Gently slide the pan back into the oven and bake.

1. Preheat oven to 200 degrees.

2. In a medium mixing bowl, combine the egg yolks, sugar and vanilla bean seeds and then whisk the mixture until it becomes fluffy and pale yellow in color. Reserve.

3. In a saucepan over medium-high heat, bring the milk and cream to a boil. Temper the egg mixture to avoid cooking the eggs, combine the tempered egg mixture with the rest of the milk and cream and then whisk the ingredients well.** Skim any bubbles from the surface of the mixture and then strain it through a fine-mesh strainer to ensure it is smooth and without lumps.

4. Pour the mixture into baking molds such as crème brûlée forms and then place them in a double water bath.† Bake the cakes in the 200-degree oven for 30-40 minutes. (You can check the cakes by shaking the mold to make sure that the surface of the cakes does not crack in the center.)

5. Remove the brûlées from the oven and let the cakes cool to room temperature.

6. To serve, sprinkle some turbinado sugar over the crème brûlées and then use a kitchen torch to melt (or caramelize) the sugar. Garnish with berries and fresh mint.

ILE FLOTANTE WITH PASSION FRUIT CARAMEL

ILE FLOTANTE

1½ cups egg whites

1 cup sugar

1⅓ teaspoons vanilla sugar

Pinch powdered dehydrated egg whites

PASSION FRUIT CARAMEL

3 cups sugar

1½ cups glucose sugar or corn syrup

1 cup heavy cream

1 vanilla bean, split, seeds removed

¾ cup passion fruit pulp

¾ cup mango pulp

1½ cups butter

CRYSTALLIZED COCONUT

¾ cup sugar

⅕ cup water

1½ cups grated coconut

BERRIES COULIS

2 cups water

1¼ cups sugar

1 pound fresh raspberries, cleaned

Serves 6

If you do not have a vapor oven, bring a small pan full of milk to a simmer over medium-low heat. Poach ½-cup portions of the egg mixture (described in step 2) in the simmering milk for 3-4 minutes, or just until they begin to grow firm. (An industry secret: You can also wrap the uncooked, ½-cup portions of egg mixture in plastic film and microwave them for 3-5 seconds.)

1. Preheat a vapor oven to 212 degrees.*

2. In a medium mixing bowl, use a whisk to whip the liquid egg whites, sugar, vanilla sugar and dehydrated egg whites until the the mixture "rises."

3. Pour the mixture into 2 half-sphere flexipans and bake in the 212-degree vapor oven for 4-5 minutes. Set aside to cool.

4. To make the caramel, combine the sugar and glucose (or corn syrup) in a saucepan over medium heat and cook the mixture for 1-2 minutes. Add the cream and vanilla and cook until the mixture reaches 255 degrees on a candy thermometer.

5. Add the passion fruit and mango pulp and cook until the mixture reaches 255 degrees on a candy thermometer. Add the butter, stir, and then remove and set aside.

6. To make the crystallized coconut, cook the sugar and water in a saucepan over medium heat until the temperature of the mixture reaches 217 degrees on a candy thermometer. When the sugar has dissolved, stir in the coconut. Place the mixture in the refrigerator to cool.

7. To make the coulis, combine the water and sugar in a saucepan and bring the mixture to a boil.

8. Add the raspberries and cook for 4 minutes. Transfer the mixture to a blender and pulse for a few minutes until the ingredients are thoroughly combined.

9. To finish, cut the top off of 1 ile flotante and remove some of the contents from the center. Add some of the coulis to the center of the ile flotante and then cover it with the second ile flotante.

10. Coat the ile flotantes with the caramel and then roll them in the crystallized coconut.

11. Place the remaining coulis in small bowls and serve alongside the ile flotante.

PASTRY CREAM

1 cup milk

2 eggs, yolks only

¼ cup sugar

2½ tablespoons pure cornstarch

SOUFFLÉ

1¼ cups cold Pastry Cream (recipe
   at right)

8 egg, yolks only

½ shot (jigger) Grand Marnier liqueur*

1¼ cups egg whites

¾ cup sugar

Pinch salt

ASSEMBLY

Melted butter, as needed

Granulated sugar, as needed

English cream (crème anglaise), to
   serve (optional)**

Serves 4

*A shot or jigger equals 1½ ounces.

***To make English cream (crème anglaise),
add 4 cups milk and 1 vanilla bean (halved
lengthwise) to a pan over medium-low heat.
Bring the milk to a soft roll and then remove
from heat. In a separate bowl, whisk 8 egg
yolks together with 1 cup granulated sugar
until the mixture turns pale yellow in color.
Add a little of the milk to the yolk mixture in a
couple of intervals, then pour the entire yolk
mixture into the pan of milk. Cook the milk
and yolk mixture over low heat, stirring until
nappe (it coats the back of a spoon).*

I recommend garnishing this dish with fruit salad and ice cream. You can also pour some English cream (crème anglaise) over the middle of the soufflé.

1. In a medium saucepan, bring the milk to a boil. Remove from heat and reserve.

2. In a large mixing bowl, combine the egg yolks, sugar and cornstarch and then whisk the ingredients until they are incorporated. Add the hot milk and transfer the entire mixture back to the saucepan on the stovetop. Bring the mixture to a boil and mix continuously. The pastry cream is cooked when it appears thick and doesn't have a floury taste.

3. Set the pastry cream in a clean container and store in the refrigerator until ready to use.

4. To a large mixing bowl, add the pastry cream, egg yolks and Grand Marnier. Use a whisk to combine the ingredients until smooth.

5. In a separate mixing bowl or in the bowl of a stand mixer, whisk the egg whites until medium peaks form. Add the sugar and continue whisking until stiff peaks form.

6. Using a spatula, fold ⅓ of the rising egg whites into the cream batter. Repeat with half of the remaining egg whites. Repeat with the rest of the egg-white mixture.

7. Preheat oven to 395 degrees.

8. Brush the inside of 4 2-inch ceramic soufflé dishes with butter. Dust the inside of the dishes with granulated sugar. Pour the soufflé batter into the prepared dishes until each is about ¾ full.

9. Bake the soufflés in the 395-degree oven for about 9 minutes. The soufflé should rise and turn golden blond in color. Serve the soufflés immediately.

10. To garnish, pour some of the English cream (crème anglaise) over the middle of the soufflé (optional).

WARM CREPES WITH GOLDEN APPLES

2 Golden Delicious apples

1 cup all-purpose flour

4 eggs

1 cup sugar

1½ cups milk

½ cup beer (such as Stella Artois)

Pinch salt

2 tablespoons butter, or as needed

Brown sugar, to serve (optional)

Whipped cream (heavy cream whisked
    together with sugar and vanilla seeds) or
    ice cream, to serve (optional)

Fruit, to serve (optional)

Serves 4

Adding a little beer to the crepe batter lightens the dough, and the yeast from the beer imparts a unique flavor that tastes great with apples.

1. Peel and core the apples but leave them whole. Slice the apples horizontally into ⅛-inch-thick "wheels" and then set them aside.

2. In a mixing bowl, whisk the flour and eggs to combine them, adding 1 egg at a time. When the mixture is smooth, add the sugar, milk, beer and salt and mix slowly to prevent lumps from forming. Let this stand for 20 minutes.

3. Add the butter to a 12-inch sauté pan and warm it over medium heat. Add 3 apple wheels and brown them on 1 side. Flip the apples and pour about ½ cup of the batter (or enough to cover the apples to the edges of the pan) over the apples. Cook each crepe for about 2 minutes, then, using a spatula or your hands, flip and cook an additional 1 minute.

4. Repeat this process and stack the finished crepes on a serving plate. Add a small amount of brown sugar between each crepe and garnish with whipped cream, ice cream, fruit or brown sugar.

PINEAPPLE UPSIDE-DOWN CRUMBLE

CRUMBLE DOUGH

½ cup butter, diced

½ cup all-purpose flour

½ cup granulated sugar

½ cup almond powder

PINEAPPLE COMPOTE

1 pineapple, skin removed and diced

½ cup brown sugar

1 piece lime peel

1⅓ tablespoons agar agar (powdered gelatin)

ASSEMBLY

English cream (crème anglaise), to serve*

Serves 8

To make English cream (crème anglaise), add 4 cups milk and 1 vanilla bean (halved lengthwise) to a pan over medium-low heat. Bring the milk to a soft roll and then remove from heat. In a separate bowl, whisk 8 egg yolks together with 1 cup granulated sugar until the mixture turns pale yellow in color. Add a little of the milk to the yolk mixture in a couple of intervals, then pour the entire yolk mixture into the pan of milk. Cook the milk and yolk mixture over low heat, stirring frequently until nappe (it coats the back of a spoon).

This recipe can be made using any in-season fruit, not just pineapple.

1. Preheat oven to 350 degrees.

2. In a large mixing bowl, combine all of the crumble dough ingredients. Press the dough into the bottom of a circular flexipan.

3. Bake the crust in the 350-degree oven for 10 minutes. Once the crust is cool, invert the crust pan and turn the dough out onto a lightly floured surface.

4. In a medium saucepan over medium heat, cook the pineapple pieces, brown sugar and lime peel. When the mixture reaches a rich, thick, syrupy consistency, add the agar agar.

5. Pour the compote mixture into a circular flexipan and place in the refrigerator to keep cold.

6. Using a 2-inch round cutter, cut out circles from the crumble dough and the pineapple compote.

7. Place a circle of crumble dough on each dessert plate. Top each circle with a circle of pineapple compote.

8. Serve lukewarm with English cream (crème anglaise).

CHOCOLATE FONDANT

1½ cups butter

1½ cups chocolate with 60 percent cocoa
   content (Valrhona or Callebaut
   chocolate)

1½ cups granulated sugar

10 eggs plus 6 egg yolks

1 cup all-purpose flour

2½ tablespoons pure cornstarch

Vanilla or pistachio ice cream, to serve

Serves 6

A classic from the Mirabelle dessert cart. High-quality chocolate is of utmost importance, so please do not compromise.

1. Set up a bain-marie (or water bath) by bringing a pot of water to a boil and setting a stainless-steel bowl over the pot of water. In the bowl, melt the butter and chocolate, stirring to combine the ingredients. Reserve.

2. In a separate mixing bowl, combine the sugar, 10 eggs and 6 egg yolks. Use a handheld mixer to cream the ingredients.

3. To the egg mixture, add the flour and cornstarch and mix them together thoroughly.

4. Using a whisk, combine the melted chocolate mixture with the egg batter until the ingredients are well incorporated.

5. Preheat oven to 375 degrees.

6. Pour the batter into 1 5-inch ring pan. Bake in the 375-degree oven for 8 minutes.

7. Serve the chocolate fondant hot and soft in the middle (like a volcano with molten lava). Serve with a scoop of vanilla or pistachio ice cream.

"NOUVEAU" PEACH TATIN

PEACH TATIN

1¼ cups white sugar

1½ tablespoons butter

5 peaches, peeled and sliced into 8 pieces
each; juice 2 of the peaches (by pureeing
in a blender)

1½ teaspoons pectin

SABLE COOKIES

6 tablespoons butter, softened

2⅓ tablespoons egg yolk

1 cup all-purpose flour

½ tablespoon dried yeast

⅓ cup sugar

Pinch salt

EXOTIC CREAM

⅛ cup mango pulp

⅛ cup coconut pulp

⅛ cup passion fruit pulp

2⅓ teaspoons sugar

1 tablespoon egg

1 tablespoon egg yolk

½ sheet gelatin

1½ tablespoons butter

ASSEMBLY

Vanilla ice cream (optional)

Serves 10

Believe me when I say that the Colorado summer peach is perhaps the best peach I have ever worked with. Absolutely delicious!

1. Preheat oven to 325 degrees.

2. To make the tatin, cook half of the sugar and all of the butter in a saucepan over medium heat until the mixture is caramelized.

3. Add the peach juice, remaining sugar, pectin and peach sections to the mixture and stir the ingredients to combine.

4. Pour the peach mixture into a round flexipan and bake in the 325-degree oven for 1 hour. Allow the tatin to cool then chill it in a refrigerator. (Leave the oven heated to 325 degrees.)

5. To make the cookies, combine the butter and egg yolk in a medium-size mixing bowl and then whisk the mixture.

6. In the bowl, add the flour and yeast and then mix the ingredients to incorporate.

7. Add the sugar and salt and then stir to combine. Set the mixture in a refrigerator for 10 minutes and then, using a rolling pin, roll the crust out to ⅛-inch thickness.

8. Using a 2-inch-diameter ring mold, cut about 10 circles from the dough. Place the circles in a round flexipan and bake them in the 325-degree oven for 15 minutes or until they are golden brown in color. Reserve.

9. To make the exotic cream, combine the fruit pulp, sugar, egg and egg yolk in a large saucepan. Place the pan over medium-high heat and bring the mixture to a boil.

10. In a separate bowl, soak the sheet of gelatin in cold water to soften it, then remove it from the water and sqeeze out excess liquid. Add the softened gelatin and butter to the pan and then allow the mixture to cool.

11. To finish, transfer the exotic cream to a pastry bag and pipe a generous dollop on top of each of the sable cookies. Add a dollop of the peach tatin and serve. (Include a scoop of vanilla ice cream of you wish.)

BELGIAN DECADENCE BEIGNET WITH CHOCOLATE, STELLA ARTOIS AND BROWN SUGAR AND BANANA COMPOTE

CHOCOLATE GANACHE

⅓ cup heavy cream

1 cup semi-sweet chocolate (such as Vahlrona 82%)

PATE BEIGNET

1½ tablespoons oil

3⅓ tablespoons Stella Artois (or other premium beer)

3⅓ tablespoons water

1 egg yolk

1 cup all-purpose flour

2 tablespoons confectioners' sugar

2 egg whites

Vegetable oil, for frying

CRISPY COCONUT MERINGUE STICKS

3⅓ teaspoons sugar

¾ cup shredded coconut

4 tablespoons egg whites

BANANA COMPOTE

2 bananas, peeled and finely diced

3 tablespoons brown sugar

1 shot (jigger) rum*

1 tablespoon butter

YOGURT SORBET

1¼ cups yogurt

½ cup sugar

1½ tablespoons glucose (no substitutions)

¾ cup water

ASSEMBLY

Chocolate sauce, to serve

Serves 4

A shot or jigger equals 1½ ounces.

1. In a medium saucepan over medium-high heat, bring the cream to a boil. Add the chocolate and stir until the chocolate is melted. Remove the mixture from heat and allow it toi cool until it forms a paste.

2. When the chocolate is cool enough to handle and has a malleable consistency, make as many 1-ounce balls as possible. Set aside.

3. To make the pate beignet, add the oil, beer and water to a mixing bowl and then combine the ingredients using a whisk.

4. Add the egg yolk to the mixture and whisk. Mix in the flour and confectioners' sugar. Reserve.

5. In a stand mixer, whip the egg whites until stiff peaks form. Fold the egg whites into the beer mixture. Set aside.

6. In a deep-fryer, preheat the vegetable oil to 350 degrees.

7. Dip the chocolate balls in the pate beignet mixture. Fry them, in batches if necessary, until they are golden brown in color (about 2 minutes). Reserve.

8. Preheat oven to 350 degrees.

9. To make the coconut meringue sticks, combine the sugar and coconut in a mixing bowl. Add the egg whites to the mixture and then blend using a handheld mixer.

10. Fill a pastry bag with the meringue mixture and pipe it onto a baking sheet in long, thin lines. Cook the meringue in the 350-degree oven for 5 minutes. Reserve.

11. To make the compote, combine the banana pieces, brown sugar, rum and butter in a saucepan and cook the mixture over medium heat until it reaches a smooth compote consistency. Reserve.

12. To make the sorbet, bring all of the sorbet ingredients to a boil in a saucepan. Pour the mixture into an ice cream machine and process according to manufacturer's directions. Place the ice cream in a freezer.

13. Place a small amount of banana compote on each of 4 dessert plates. Place the pate beignets over the compote. Drizzle chocolate sauce on the side of the plate and add a scoop of the yogurt sorbet to the plate. Place a coconut meringue stick in the beignet to garnish.

SUGAR TART FROM BELGIUM

SUGAR DOUGH

1¼ cups all-purpose flour

10 tablespoons granulated sugar

9 tablespoons butter

1 egg yolk

¼ cup water

SUGAR CREAM

2 eggs

½ cup sugar

½ cup brown sugar

2½ tablespoons almond powder

½ cup heavy cream

Serves 8

Take a trip to Belgium with this classic tart. It's great with afternoon coffee or tea.

1. In a mixing bowl, combine the flour and sugar and then stir them together. Cut in the butter and mix by hand.

2. Add the egg yolk and water and knead the mixture with your hands until the dough reaches a soft-but-firm consistency.

3. Chill the dough in a refrigerator for 1 hour.

4. To make the sugar cream filling, combine the eggs, sugar, brown sugar, almond powder and cream in a mixing bowl. Set aside.

5. Preheat oven to 390 degrees.

6. Roll the sugar dough out to ⅛-inch thickness. Place the dough across a 10-inch tart pan. Press the dough down into the pan. Blind bake the dough for 5 minutes in the 390-degree oven.

7. Reduce the oven temperature to 375 degrees.

8. Pour the sugar cream mixture into the crust and bake in the 375-degree oven for 20 minutes.

9. Remove the tart from the tart pan and allow it to cool. (It is delicious served a little bit warm.)

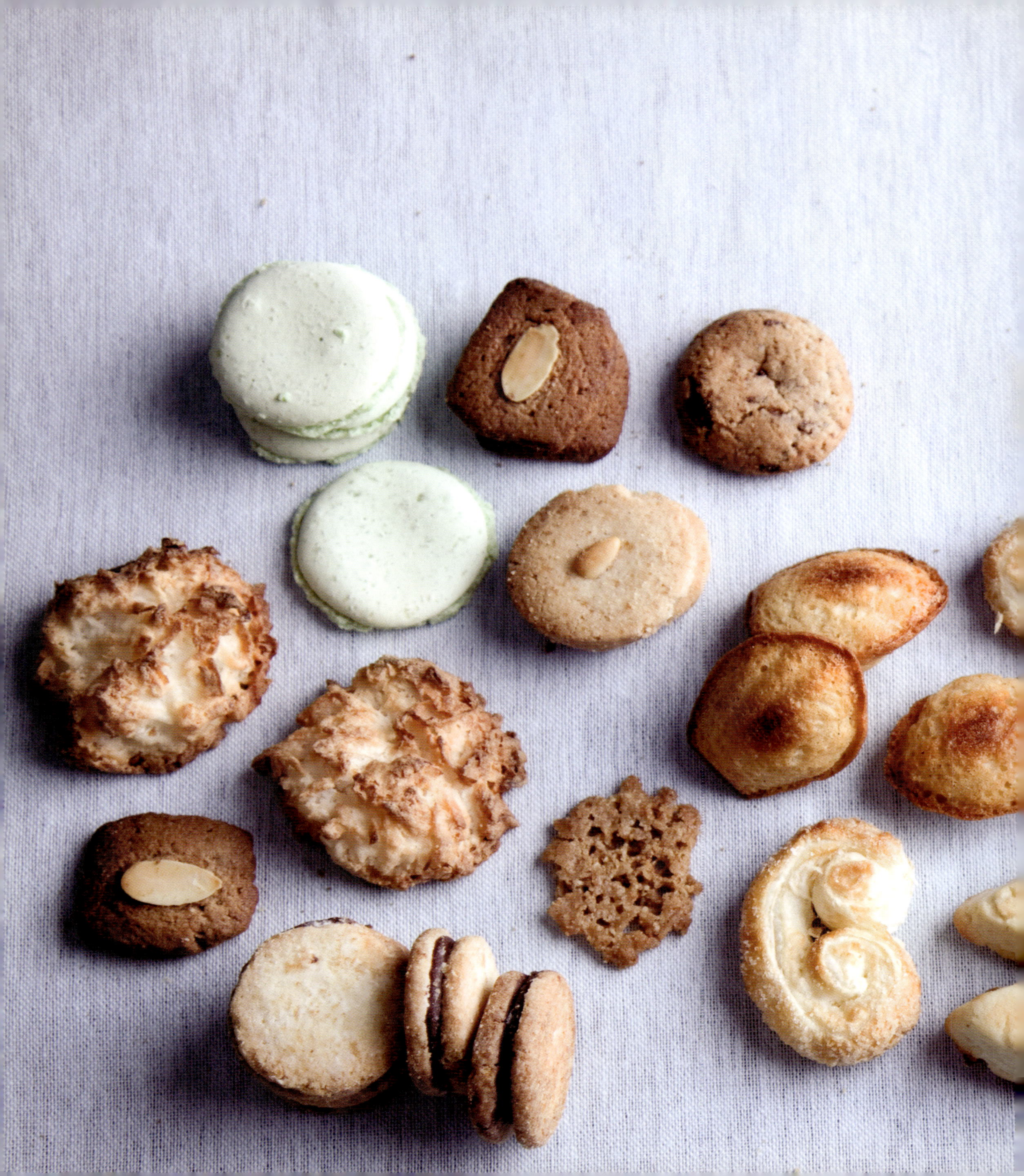

LEMON COOKIES

⅓ cup egg yolks
¾ cup sugar
Zest of 4 lemons
1⅔ tablespoons
   lemon juice
⅔ cup egg whites
¼ cup all-purpose
   flour
¼ cup cornstarch

Yields 25 cookies

1. Preheat oven to 300 degrees.

2. Blend the egg yolks, ½ cup of the sugar, the lemon zest and lemon juice. Reserve.

3. Blend the egg whites and ¼ cup of the sugar until the egg whites are soft.

4. Using a mixer, combine the two mixtures, adding the flour and cornstarch at the end.

5. Using a pastry bag, form the dough into ½-inch-diameter circles (similar to macaroons) on a greased baking sheet.

6. Bake in a 300-degree oven for 30 minutes.

COCONUT ROCHERS

1 egg white
2 tablespoons warm
   water
1¼ cups powdered
   sugar
2¼ cups shredded
   coconut

Yields 25 cookies

1. Preheat oven to 375 degrees.

2. Blend the egg white with the warm water.

3. Slowly add the sugar and then the coconut.(If the dough seems too thick, add another tablespoon of water.)

4. Form the dough into small circle shapes on a greased baking sheet.

5. Bake in a 375-degree oven for 25 minutes.

WHITE CHOCOLATE BROWNIES

10½ ounces white
   chocolate
1 cup butter,
   softened
4 eggs
⅓ teaspoon salt
1½ cups all-purpose
   flour
1 teaspoon vanilla
   powder
⅔ teaspoon dry
   yeast
1 cup grilled
   pistachios
1 cup walnuts
1½ cups white
   chocolate chips

Serves 8

1. Preheat oven to 300 degrees.

2. Set up a bain-marie and soften the white chocolate. (For instructions on setting up a bain-marie, see step 1 of recipe on page 126.)

3. Using a mixer, combine the softened chocolate, softened butter, eggs, salt, flour, vanilla powder, yeast, pistachios, walnuts and chocolate chips.

4. Place the dough in a greased, deep-sided baking pan.

5. Bake in a 300-degree oven for 35 minutes.

BROWN SUGAR COOKIES

2 1/3 cups all-
   purpose flour
1 egg yolk
⅞ cup butter
⅔ cup brown sugar
1 pinch cinnamon
1 pinch baking
   soda
1 star anise

Serves 6-8

1. Preheat oven to 375 degrees.

2. Pour the flour into a bowl and then add the rest of the ingredients (except for the egg yolk) to the center of the pile of flour. Mix well.

3. Form the dough into a baguette shape. Reserve overnight in a refrigerator.

4. Cut the dough into ½-inch circles. Place the circles on a greased baking sheet and bake them in a 375-degree oven for 10 minutes.

5. Remove the cookies from the oven, brush them with the egg yolk and then cook them again for 2 minutes.

SABLES WITH EARL GREY TEA GANACHE

SABLES

1⅓ cups butter

1¾ cups sugar

¾ cup almond powder

4 cups all-purpose flour

1 cup crystal sugar

2 egg yolks

EARL GREY TEA GANACHE

⅛ cup water

1 tablespoon glucose sugar

3⅓ tablespoons Earl Grey tea (dry)

½ cup cream

8¾ ounces couverture noire (extra bitter chocolate), melted

¼ cup butter, melted

Yields 40 cookies

1. Preheat oven to 375 degrees.

2. To make the sables, combine the butter and sugar using a mixer. Add the almond powder then the flour and mix well.

3. Roll the sable dough into a baguette shape and then roll it in the crystal sugar. Reserve the dough in a refrigerator for 2 hours.

4. Cut the sable dough into ½-inch circles and then place the circles on a greased baking sheet.

5. Bake in a 375-degree oven for 10-15 minutes. Reserve.

6. To make the ganache, boil the water with the glucose and then remove from heat.

7. Add the tea and let it steep for 5 minutes.

8. Pour the cream into a bowl and then strain the tea mixture into the bowl with the cream. Add the melted chocolate.

9. Let the mixture cool to 97 degrees and then add the melted butter.

10. Using a pastry bag, squeeze some of the ganache onto the tops of half of the sables and then press the rest of the sables onto the ganache-covered sables (like making sandwiches).

PISTACHIO MACAROONS

4 cups almond powder

9 cups powdered sugar

1 egg white plus additional

1½ cups egg whites*

½ cup pistachio paste

Serves 6-8

*It is always better to use egg whites that are 2-3 days old when making macaroons. You will obtain a better final result.

1. Preheat oven to 275 degrees.

2. Using a mixer, combine the almond powder with 4 cups of the sugar. Add the 1 egg white and pistachio paste and then mix well. Reserve.

3. Combine the 1½ cups of egg whites with 5 cups of the sugar and warm the mixture in a bain-marie, stirring until it reaches a temperature of 122 degrees. (For instructions on setting up a bain-marie, see step 1 of recipe on page 126.) Remove the mixture (known as "meringue suisse") from the bain-marie and let it cool, stirring until the egg whites are cold.

4. In a mixing bowl, combine the two mixtures a little bit at a time. Using a pastry bag, form the new mixture into several ½-inch circles on a greased baking sheet.

5. Let the macaroons stand at room temperature for 20 minutes to develop a crust.

6. Bake in a 275-degree oven for 5-6 minutes.

PRALINE COOKIES

½ cup almond powder
1¾ cups brown sugar
¾ cup all-purpose flour
½ cup butter, softened
2 tablespoons water
3 tablespoons praline paste

Serves 6-8

1. Preheat oven to 300 degrees.

2. Using a mixer, combine all of the ingredients.

3. Form the dough into small balls and then arrange them on a greased baking sheet.

4. Bake in a 300-degree oven for 10-12 minutes.

CROUSTILLONS

4 cups all-purpose flour
1 cup sugar
2 tablespoons yeast
3 eggs
1 pinch powdered cinnamon
1⅓ cups milk
Powdered sugar, as needed

Serves 6-8

1. Preheat a deep fryer to 385 degrees.

2. Mix the flour with the sugar. Add the yeast, mixed with half of the milk, to the center of the pile of flour and sugar. Beat the ingredients together until the dough is soft. Add the eggs and cinnamon. Reserve for 30 minutes.

3. Place spoonfuls of the dough in a 385-degree deep-fryer and fry them for 3-4 minutes.

4. Take out the croustillons and drain them on paper towels. Sprinkle powdered sugar over them and serve warm.

SMALL FLEMISH BOOTS

SUGAR DOUGH
2 cups all-purpose flour
1 pinch salt
⅔ cup sugar
1 egg
½ cup butter, softened

FRUIT MIXTURE
⅓ cup sugar
2 egg yolks
¼ cup all-purpose flour (plus more as needed)
⅞ cup milk, warmed
2 tablespoons kirsch
⅛ cup cherry confit, chopped
10 almonds, chopped

Yields 10 cookies

1. Preheat oven to 400-450 degrees.

2. Tamiser (or sift) the flour into a bowl to remove any lumps. Add all of the sugar dough ingredients to the center of the pile of flour.

3. Using a mixer, combine the ingredients and then place in a refrigerator for 30 minutes.

4. Mix the sugar with the egg yolks, then add the flour and warm milk. Bring the mixture to a boil, stirring constantly.

5. Remove from heat, add the kirsch and then let the mixture cool. Stir and then add the cherry confit.

6. Grease 10 small pastry forms and then dust them with flour. Place some sugar dough in each form and top with the fruit mixture and almonds.

7. Bake in a 400- to 450-degree oven for 12 minutes.

SAINT-NICOLAS SPÉCULOOS

1⅛ cups butter, softened
1¾ cups brown sugar
2 eggs
1 pinch each of cinnamon, muscade, star anise, ginger and cocoa
1 whole clove, chopped
1 pinch salt
2¾ cups all-purpose flour
1 teaspoon dry yeast
Almonds, blanched and sliced, as needed

Serves 6-8

1. Preheat oven to 325 degrees.

2. In a terrine (or mold), mix the ingredients in this order: butter, sugar, eggs, spices, salt, flour and yeast. Reserve in a refrigerator until the next day.

3. Divide the dough into small peaces. Cut the pieces into ½-inch-long-rectangles and then decorate each with a slice of blanched almond.

4. Bake in a 325-degree oven for 6 minutes.

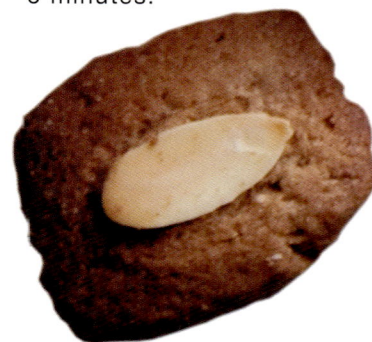

HEART COOKIES (PALMIER)

10½ ounces pastry dough
4 egg yolks
½ cup sugar

Yields 25 cookies

1. Preheat oven to 350 degrees.

2. Place the dough on a clean, flat surface and brush some of the egg yolks onto the dough.

3. Sprinkle some of the sugar over the top of the dough.

4. Roll the dough from the top to the center and from the bottom to the center (forming a heart shape).

5. Brush the dough again with egg yolks and roll it in sugar.

6. Cut the dough into ½-inch-thick shapes.

7. Reserve the cut dough in a refrigerator for 20 minutes.

8. Bake in a 350-degree oven for 8 minutes or until the cookies are golden brown in color.

CHOCOLATE CHIP COOKIES

¾ cup unsalted butter
⅔ cup granulated sugar
1¼ cup dark brown sugar
2 eggs
1 teaspoon baking soda
1 teaspoon vanilla extract
2¾ cups all-purpose flour
2 cups chocolate chips

Yields 12-14 cookies

1. Preheat oven to 350 degrees.

2. Cream the butter and gradually beat in the sugar. Beat in the eggs one by one, followed by the baking soda, vanilla and flour. Add the chocolate chips and stir them into the mixture.

3. Use a small spoon to portion out quarter-sized lumps of dough onto a greased baking sheet, leaving 2-3 inches between each cookie.

4. Bake in a 350-degree oven for 10 minutes. (Store cookies in a box to keep them fresh.)

CHOCOLATE TRUFFLES

10 ounces bittersweet chocolate
½ cup whipping cream
½ cup and 4 tablespoons clarified butter
⅓ cup cocoa powder

Yields 20-30 truffles

1. In a saucepan over medium heat, combine the chocolate and cream, stirring the mixture constantly until the chocolate has melted.

2. Bring the mixture to a boil, remove from heat and then let it cool.

3. Pour the chocolate mixture into the bowl of a stand mixer and beat at high speed for 3-4 minutes, or until the mixture turns light and fluffy. Gradually add the butter.

4. Line a baking sheet with waxed paper.

5. Spread the chocolate mixture at a thickness of ½ inch on the lined baking sheet. Refrigerate the mixture for at least 2 hours.

6. Cut the chocolate mixture into ½-inch squares and then roll them between the palms of your hands for form balls. Roll the balls in the cocoa powder with a fork. Store the truffles in a refrigerator.

INDEX

potato-crusted alaskan halibut with julienne of
    snow peas **78**
halibut with salsa of pears, cucumber, carrot and pinot
    noir reduction **80**
dover sole meuniere mirabelle **82**
sauté of monkfish on a bed of belgian endive in stella
    artois beer sauce **84**
hoegaarden-steamed salmon with vegetable tempura
    and spicy tomato coulis **86**

SHRIMP
sautéed gulf shrimp salad **46**
thai papaya salad with sautéed california prawns **48**

SOLE
dover sole meuniere mirabelle **82**

SORBETS
"our friend maria's" lemon meringue tart **113**
belgian decadence beignet with chocolate, stella artois
    and brown sugar and banana compote **131**

SOUFFLÉS
grand marnier soufflé **120**

SOUP
lobster bisque **38**
corn chowder **40**
cold gazpacho soup **42**
chilled melon soup with diced prosciutto ham **44**

SPINACH
dover sole meuniere mirabelle **82**
colorado rack of lamb "grand daddy style" with garlic
    mashed potatoes **104**

SQUASH
chanterelle ragout with acorn squash ravioli **65**
grilled tuna with roasted vegetables, balsamic
    lemon vinaigrette **74**
hoegaarden-steamed salmon with vegetable tempura
    and spicy tomato coulis **86**
duck with butternut squash and soy sauce reduction **92**

SNOW PEA
potato-crusted alaskan halibut with julienne of
    snow peas **78**

TARTARE
buffalo tartare **22**

TARTS
tomato tart **30**
"our friend maria's" lemon meringue tart **113**
pear tart "moeulleux" **114**
sugar tart from belgium **132**

TEA
sables with earl grey tea ganache **137**

TOMATO
tomato tart **30**
cold gazpacho soup **42**
artichoke salad **56**
crusty crust with goat cheese and fruit compote, frisée
    salad with abbaye de leffe orange vinaigrette **59**
a summer pizza feuillet **60**
spicy pasta with tomatoes and arugula **62**
hoegaarden-steamed salmon with vegetable tempura
    and spicy tomato coulis **86**
fresh free-range chicken with vegetable gateau, tomato
    and bell pepper jus **96**

TROUT
colorado trout with lemon jam **76**

TUNA
grilled tuna with roasted vegetables, balsamic
    lemon vinaigrette **74**

VEAL
veal carpaccio with cilantro herb salad **26**
grilled free-range veal chop with broccoli mousseline,
    morel sauce **100**

WALNUT
white chocolate brownies **136**

WINE
duck breast with wine-poached pears in red wine and
    milk-poached celery root mousseline **90**
herb parmesan-crusted elk tenderloin with cream-
    poached salsify, "red" yukon gold potatoes and port wine
    reduction **94**
grilled beef tenderloin with braised endives and
    pommes galette **98**
grilled free-range veal chop with broccoli mousseline,
    morel sauce **100**

ZUCCHINI
crusty crust with goat cheese and fruit compote, frisée
    salad with abbaye de leffe orange vinaigrette **59**
a summer pizza feuillet **60**
asian infused jumbo sautéed scallops **68**
colorado trout with lemon jam **76**
fresh free-range chicken with vegetable gateau, tomato
    and bell pepper jus **96**
roasted colorado rack of lamb with zucchini and
    artichoke ballotine and garlic emulsion **103**
stella artois-marinated flank steak **108**

MARIA PEDOT

SEBASTIEN SCHMITT

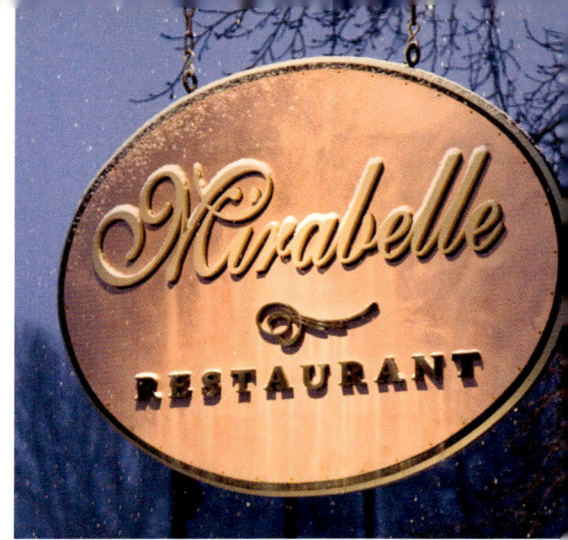

MIRABELLE RESTAURANT

DANIEL JO